English To

V. J. Cook

OXFORD UNIVERSITY PRESS

Oxford University Press, Walton Street, Oxford OX2 6DP
OXFORD LONDON GLASGOW
NEW YORK TORONTO MELBOURNE WELLINGTON
IBADAN NAIROBI DAR ES SALAAM LUSAKA CAPE TOWN
KUALA LUMPUR SINGAPORE JAKARTA HONG KONG TOKYO
DELHI BOMBAY CALCUTTA MADRAS KARACHI

ISBN 0 19 453280 1
© Vivian Cook, 1974

First published 1974
Third impression 1977

All rights reserved. No part of this publication may be reproduced, stored in a retrieval system, or transmitted, in any form or by any means, electronic, mechanical, photocopying, recording or otherwise, without the prior permission of Oxford University Press.

This book is sold subject to the condition that it shall not, by way of trade or otherwise, be lent, re-sold, hired out, or otherwise circulated without the publisher's prior consent in any form of binding or cover other than that in which it is published and without a similar condition including this condition being imposed on the subsequent purchaser.

Printed in Great Britain by Robert MacLehose & Co. Ltd
Printers to the University of Glasgow

CONTENTS

		Page
Introduction		v
Topic 1	Teaching	9
Topic 2	Holidays	21
Topic 3	The Supernatural	34
Topic 4	Houses	45
Topic 5	Food	57
Topic 6	Speech	69
Topic 7	Jobs	81
Topic 8	Sports & Games	93
Topic 9	Fashion & Pop	105
Topic 10	The Arts	116

ACKNOWLEDGEMENTS

The publisher and author wish to thank the following for their permission to use extracts from copyright material:
Thomson Holidays Ltd (*Thomson Skytours: Lakes, Mountains and Fjords*); Clarksons (*Clarksons Cruisejets 1973*); Pontinental (*Pontinental Summer 1973*); Unilever Ltd. (*Careers in Unilever 1973*); The Times (*Australia v Indonesia in the Federation Cup* by Rex Bellamy); Condé Nast Publications Ltd. (*Summer Fashion* from *Brides and Setting Up Home*).

They also wish to thank the following for permission to use photographs on the pages quoted: British Airways, 87 (bottom); British Broadcasting Corporation, 122 (bottom); British Film Institute, 122 (top), 123 (top); British Tourist Authority, 28 (top); Camera Press, 16 (top), 17, 27, 28 (bottom), 52, 110 (left), 111; J. Allan Cash, 64; Central Office of Information, 15; Central Press, 100 (bottom); Keystone Press Agency, 16 (bottom), 39, 63, 74, 75, 87 (top), 88, 99, 100 (top), 110 (right), 123 (bottom); Shakespeare Birthplace Trust Library, 40 (bottom); Society for Psychical Research, 40 (top); Wates Ltd, 51.

INTRODUCTION

The aim of *English Topics* is to equip the foreign learner of English with the ability to take an active part in conversations in English. The course is intended to be used with students at intermediate to advanced levels; in particular it is suitable as a preparation for the First Certificate of Cambridge University (formerly the Lower Certificate). The course is planned to get the student actively speaking and listening in the classroom. It consists of a variety of materials, all with the purpose of making the student eager to express himself in English and to understand what other people are saying. It is organized around ten topics, ranging from 'Sport' to 'The Supernatural', from 'Teaching' to 'Pop Music and Fashion'. These ten are known to be frequently discussed by English people and are selected so that a variety of beliefs and opinions can be expressed about them. The teaching material in each topic is organized in the following way:

Background material
Usually this contains a descriptive passage or extract about the topic; in the case of 'Food' for instance it is recipes given by foreign students; in the case of 'Holidays' it is extracts from holiday brochures. This provides the student with some of the structural items and vocabulary used when talking about the topic. Then there comes some brief factual information, mostly based on England, and some points arising from the passage and the factual information for the student to consider. One way in which the teacher can use this material is to ask the students to read it the night before the class and to decide what they themselves think about the points to consider. Then the teacher can start the class by asking the students for their reactions.

Dialogues
Each topic has two short scripted conversations, each with a different purpose. *Dialogue 1* is for general work in the class-

Introduction

room. The teacher either reads it aloud to the students or plays them the tape. Then he makes them repeat it in small sections, either individually or in chorus, and he and the class discuss any points that arise; at the end of the conversation there are some suggestions for 'talking points' that the teacher can use as a basis for this. *Dialogue 2* is for reading aloud. The students first read it silently, then choose parts and read it aloud. After this they discuss anything that interests them in the conversation; again a list of 'talking points' is supplied. Finally, if they have the tape, they can listen to the recording of the conversation.

Activities
Each topic contains a number of 'activities' to provoke the student into using English. Usually a topic has five of these. *Activity 1* is a questionnaire which asks the students to answer several questions about the topic; the students can fill it in at home or do it in the classroom. As well as practice in comprehension, the questionnaire provides a starting-point for classroom discussion and argument. The teacher can, for example, count up on the blackboard how many students have answered in one way or another, and get the minority, or indeed the majority, to justify their views. Alternatively the teacher can challenge the students' views or he can contrast them with those of English people; many other approaches will also lead to useful classroom discussion and exploitation. *Activity 2* is often a 'case-study': the students are given information about an imaginary situation and then have to solve some of its problems and act out some of its happenings. In 'Teaching', for instance, the students are given a brief portrait of a school including biographies of teachers and pupils; they have to try to solve some problems in the school and to act out some situations in which the characters find themselves. *Activity 3* varies from topic to topic. *Activity 4* usually consists of photographs linked to the topic; in 'Sport', for example, there are photographs of a famous tennis player, a champion skier, and a motor-racing crash. The student is asked to talk about the photographs: to give him some help, brief hints are given under each photo. *Activity 5* provides a list of short talks; the students prepare and give talks lasting two to three minutes on one aspect or another of the topic.

Introduction

Listening Passages
Each topic has two listening passages. *Passage 1* is scripted and has multiple-choice questions. The students first listen to the passage, either from the tape or from the teacher's reading aloud. Then they look at the questions and listen to the passage again as many times as the teacher or the students think necessary to attempt all the questions. They discuss the content of the passage, a list of discussion points being given. Finally they look at the written text. Alternatively the passage can be treated as reading comprehension, when the students read it silently before answering the questions. *Passage 2* is an extract from a live recording of English speakers speaking spontaneously; the exercise that goes with it is one in which the student must agree or disagree with several statements about the passage. Again the students listen to the passage from the tape or hear their teacher reading it before seeing the exercise; they listen again as often as necessary and discuss the passage, possibly using the discussion points suggested. Finally they see the written transcript. There are usually two versions of this, either or both of which may be used. One is simply the unedited transcript of what was actually said; the other is a slightly edited version. Some teachers may prefer to use the edited version because they feel it is easier for their class; others may prefer the unedited transcript because it provides practice in comprehending real spontaneous English. If the teacher does not have the tapes but has to read the transcript aloud, it is probably better for him to use the edited version. Finally, after the passages there are some suggestions for written work – essays, letters, conversations, and so on.

It is not intended that the topics should necessarily be gone through in the order in which they appear; instead the teacher should choose those which are best suited to the needs and interests of his class, and teach them in the order he feels suits them best. Similarly with the material in each topic the teacher is free to select those parts which he feels are most suitable and to teach them in the order he likes, to suit the mood, pace, and reactions of the class. While it may be likely that the 'Background material' is best introduced first and the 'Suggestions for written work' last, the conversations, activities, and listening passages in each topic should be combined in any way that suits the teaching situation. *English Topics* is intended

Introduction

to be used flexibly; nothing could defeat its object of involving the students in the spontaneous use of English more easily than going through each topic in a mechanical unvarying manner.

English Topics is then based on two assumptions about language teaching. One is that many people study a foreign language because they want to talk to other people about things that interest them; they do not want an academic knowledge of the language nor do they want simply to be able to use English in purely practical exchanges in shops and restaurants: they want rather to express their own ideas to people in English and to be able to understand those of others. They hope to acquire the ability to inform, to contradict, to argue, to discuss, to hear and say things they have not said or heard before, to get a particular reaction from the listener, and to be aware of what reaction a speaker is hoping to provoke: in short they need a flexible ability to communicate in English in the give-and-take situation of real conversation. The second assumption behind *English Topics* concerns language learning and is that the ability to communicate is best acquired by actually communicating: you learn to understand spontaneous speech by listening to spontaneous speech; you learn to speak spontaneously by speaking spontaneously. So activities which make the student a passive observer and parrot of other people's sentences and opinions are not so effective as those which involve him actively. All the different parts of *English Topics* provide opportunities for the student to understand and use speech himself. He is expected throughout to use the book as the spring-board for expressing his own opinions and his own thoughts; to react to what he encounters rather than to accept it passively.

TOPIC ONE
TEACHING

Background Text

Education in England

In England children go to school between the ages of five and sixteen. Most children attend 'State' schools, which are free. Much of the responsibility for education is taken by local governments rather than by the national government, so each area usually differs slightly from the general pattern. The state system is divided into three levels: primary schools for children from five to eleven; secondary schools for children from eleven to at least sixteen; and further or higher education for those who have left school.

Primary schools have changed greatly in recent years under the influence of new theories about child development and new ideas about what they should learn. A typical classroom, such as the one shown on page 15, no longer has rows of desks facing the teacher; instead the room is divided into 'areas' for particular activities, where the children can work alone or in groups under the guidance of the teacher.

State secondary schools fall into three main types: secondary modern, grammar, and comprehensive. Until recently children were selected at about eleven to go to secondary modern or grammar schools, the secondary modern school being intended for the more practical child, the grammar school for the more academic. In the nineteen-sixties the national government tried to make all secondary schools 'comprehensive', that is to say, accept all the children that live in their district rather than select only a few. Many areas of England have now adopted this system and no longer have 'selection'.

Higher education has several branches: colleges of education that mostly prepare students to be teachers, polytechnics that usually prepare students for some kind of career, and universities. Virtually all higher education is selective, usually depending on how well a student does in G.C.E. 'A' level (the General Certificate of Education, 'Advanced' level), taken at about eighteen.

Topic One

Facts about English Education in 1972
i) Secondary modern schools in England and Wales had 1,085,000 pupils, grammar schools 540,000, and comprehensives 1,337,000.
ii) The proportion of pupils to teachers was 26 to 1 in primary schools, 19 to 1 in secondary moderns, and 17 to 1 in grammar schools.
iii) The average size of a class in a primary school was 31 pupils, in a secondary modern 25, and in a grammar school 26.

Points to Consider
a) What are the chief differences and similarities between the English state system of education and that in your country?
b) Is there selection in your country's educational system? At school? At university? What kinds of selection do you approve of?
c) What proportion of pupils to teachers do you feel is best?

Dialogue 1 *Priorities in Education*
Listen to this conversation between three friends; then repeat it in small sections and discuss the points that arise.

ANN: I think it's quite ridiculous spending money on a select few and ignoring everyone else.
JAMES: What are you talking about?
ANN: The fact that universities get plenty of money and primary schools get none.
JAMES: That isn't really true.
SARA: In any case universities need more money – for equipment, for libraries, and so on.
ANN: And primary schools need it for books, teachers and so on.
SARA: Yes, but universities don't just teach; they also do research.
ANN: That's the trouble: they care more for their research than for their students.
JAMES: Well they've done a lot of useful research in the past.
ANN: That still doesn't mean they should get the lion's share of the money.
JAMES: I didn't say that. In fact I agree that the proportion's wrong.
SARA: Well I don't. If we're to compete in the modern world, we have to keep up the standards of our universities, and that means spending money.

Teaching

Talking Points
a) What *should* determine how much money is spent on the different kinds of education?
b) What is the function of higher education? Acquiring knowledge? Learning skills? Being trained for a job?
c) How important is money to education? What difference do beautiful new buildings and well-paid teachers make?

Dialogue 2 *Exams*
First read this conversation between two students silently. Then choose parts and read the conversation aloud. Finally discuss any points that arise.
BRENDA: I know I'm going to fail the exam.
PATRICK: Oh?
BRENDA: It's not that I haven't worked. This term I've done nothing but sit in the library.
PATRICK: In fact you've been most unfriendly.
BRENDA: Well I'm scared of failing. You see I'm one of those people who panic in exams: all my thoughts seem to go out of my head.
PATRICK: That's what's wrong with the system, isn't it? You study for three years and you take an exam that lasts three hours. What happens in the exam is what counts, not the rest of the three years.
BRENDA: Yes. Some people can do exams, some can't; I'm one of the ones who can't.
PATRICK: Well what does that prove? Passing an exam just shows you're the kind of person who can pass exams; it doesn't show that you're clever, that you work hard, or anything else at all.

Talking Points
a) How much studying should a student do? Which is more important – working in the library or meeting fellow students?
b) What are the justifications for a three-hour written exam? What does this kind of exam actually measure?
c) How could exams be improved? By having them more often? By using multiple-choice questions (like those on page 18)? In other ways?

Topic One

Activity 1 *Teaching Questionnaire*
Tick the answers that you agree with most.
1. What age should children start school?
a) 3 to 4
b) 5 to 6
c) 7 to 8
2. If you had to make a choice would you send your children to
a) selective schools?
b) comprehensive schools?
c) no school at all?
3. How much should parents have to pay for their children's education?
a) nothing
b) a little
c) what they can afford
d) the full cost
4. Should decisions about children's education be made by
a) the government?
b) the school-teachers?
c) the parents?
d) the children themselves?
e) a combination of any of these?
5. If a child is unsuccessful at school is this chiefly the fault of
a) the parents?
b) the teachers?
c) the child?
d) none of these?
6. Which of these subjects should be compulsory for all pupils? (Sport and religion are compulsory in England.)
a) sport
b) religion
c) politics
d) mathematics
e) a foreign language
f) another subject not mentioned here
7. When the child first goes to school which of these areas are most important?
a) reading, writing and arithmetic (the three Rs)
b) social adaptation to other children and to society
c) mental growth of the individual child
d) sport
8. When someone is a 'good' teacher is it because
a) he knows his subject?

b) he knows his pupils?
c) the pupils like him?
d) none of these?
9. If a child had done something you regard as very wrong and you were his teacher, would you
a) hit him?
b) talk to him severely?
c) make him do extra work?
d) keep him at school after the other pupils have left?
e) make him stand up in front of the class and describe what he had done?
f) do none of these?
10. For which of the following reasons would you want to have higher education?
a) training for a job
b) interesting social life
c) opportunity to acquire knowledge
d) chance to serve society
e) better job prospects
f) other reasons

Activity 2 *Silford Comprehensive School*
The school is located in a poor district where many people are unemployed. Many of the children's parents have grave problems with money, housing, and employment and so cannot take much interest in their children's education. The school buildings are old but solid, rather like the one shown in photo 3 on page 16.

The Staff
John Bentley, the headmaster. He is in his late fifties; he is interested in sport and doesn't believe in modern 'nonsense'. He takes a real interest in his pupils, many of whom keep in touch with him for years after they leave.
Betty Newham, the English teacher. She is in her mid-thirties and believes strongly in the importance of creative writing to develop the individual. Mostly the pupils like her.
Michael Blake, the maths teacher. He is in his twenties and has only recently come down from university. He is serious and quiet and gives the impression that mathematics is the only important school subject. Some of the pupils find him cold.

Topic One

The Pupils

Peter Allen is fifteen and intelligent but is bored with school. He likes motorbikes, plays the guitar, and belongs to a youth club. He doesn't know what he wants to do when he leaves school.

Helen Windsor is sixteen, quiet and pretty, and about average in her schoolwork. She seldom goes out and doesn't have many friends outside her family.

George Summers is sixteen and very good at maths. He lives alone with his father and is often absent from school. His chief interest is football. He appears rather tense and nervous.

Their Problems

Discuss how the following problems might be solved.

1. George Summers looks rather pale and thin; his clothes are torn; he never has any money for school excursions. What should the staff do?
2. Michael Blake has been offered a job in industry at twice his present salary. What do you advise?
3. The staff suspect that Peter Allen, and possibly other pupils, are taking dangerous drugs. What should they do?
4. The school have been given some money to spend. Should they spend it on sports equipment, on a tape-recorder, or on painting some of the classrooms?
5. Helen Windsor's parents want her to go to university; the staff think that this would mean too much work for her; Helen doesn't really mind what she does. What do you suggest?

Situations

Take the parts of the different characters and act out the following situations.

1. Michael Blake has taken Peter Allen to see the headmaster because he claims that Peter hit him. Peter says it was an accident.
2. Peter Allen wants to take Helen to the pictures; George objects as he wanted to go to a football match with Peter the same evening.
3. The headmaster has asked to see George Summer's father to find out what is wrong and how George can be helped.
4. George Summers has twisted his ankle playing football. Helen and Peter help him walk to the staffroom where the staff have to deal with the situation.

Teaching

Activity 3 *The End of Term Report*
Fill out this report on a term's work either for one of the pupils of Silford School or for yourself as a child.

Name of School:	
Pupil's name:	Class:
English Geography Sport Music Mathematics History	
Behaviour in school:	
General comments:	

Activity 4 *Photographs*

Photo 1   *A Primary School Classroom*
Describe what is going on in this classroom. What do you think of this kind of teaching? Is it more work or less work for the teachers?

1

Topic One

Photo 2 *A Classroom*
Describe what is happening here. In what ways is this classroom different from that in photo 1? Which would you prefer?

Photo 3 *A Playground*
Describe what the children are doing and their school. What is the value of this kind of play? What kinds of problems might there be in this school?

Photo 4 *The University of Sussex*
Describe the students and what they are doing. Would you like to study in this kind of environment?

2

3

Teaching

4

Activity 5 *Short Talks*
Prepare and give a short talk lasting two to three minutes on one of the following topics.
  1. Exams.
  2. My worst experience at school.
  3. The teacher I liked best.
  4. My favourite school subject.
  5. School food.
  6. The teacher's responsibility to his pupils.
  7. Is education the most important way of changing society?
  8. The importance of higher education.
  9. Learning a foreign language.
  10. Teachers are born, not made.

Listening *My First School*
Passage 1 Listen to this story about the speaker's first school. Then look at the questions. Listen to the story again as many times as you need to answer the questions. Then discuss the points that arise and look at the written text.

17

Topic One

Questions
Tick the answer that fits the passage best.
1. The speaker finds it difficult
   a) to remember his first school.
   b) to judge the truth of his memories.
   c) to talk about his memories.
2. He a) knew then   that the lady was the headmistress.
       b) knows now
       c) guesses now
3. During his first day at school he remembers children
   a) learning arithmetic.
   b) learning geography.
   c) singing.
4. a) The teachers   seemed frightening.
   b) The children
   c) The activities
5. The chief reason why he remembers these activities is that
   a) he did them every day.
   b) he understood them.
   c) he didn't do them every day.

Discussion Points
a) What do you think really happened on the occasions he describes? What was the purpose of these activities?
b) In what ways should parents and teachers make the first day at school easier for the child? Were they successful in this case?
c) Are your earliest memories pleasant or unpleasant? How much can you trust them?

Written Text
It is sometimes hard to tell whether the first things that one remembers are true or false. In particular I am never certain whether my memories of the first school I went to are genuine or are the products of sheer imagination. I seem to remember on the first day being in an enormous room, full of mothers and children, desks and blackboards, papers and piles of strange objects, and a fierce-looking lady, who must, I suppose, have been the headmistress, looking down at me from a great height and talking interminably. Then suddenly I was in another room where a teacher was pointing at a blackboard and the children were chanting 'Two twos are four; two threes are six . . .' I had no idea what these things meant but they all

Teaching

seemed very important and slightly frightening. School was a mysterious place where almost anything could happen. Did we really spend a day looking for plants on a rubbish dump? Did we spend a whole morning standing on the pavement outside the school counting the number of fire-engines and ambulances that passed? At the time I didn't know why we did these things nor did my slightly worried parents. Perhaps it was the very unusualness of these activities that made them stick in my mind; the ordinary things we did every day are long since forgotten.

Listening Passage 2 *School Food*

This passage consists of a live talk on a prepared topic. The speaker is Mrs Pam Cook who has taught at a variety of levels in the English educational system. The topic she chose from the list on page 17 was 'School Food' and she decided to tell an anecdote about 'dinner duty'. (In English schools the teachers often have to take turns to supervise the pupils at lunch. This is called 'dinner duty'.) A teacher was forcing a small child to eat her lunch and neither Mrs Cook nor the child found the experience very pleasant.

Listen to the talk at least once before looking at the exercise. Listen to the talk again as many times as you need to do the exercise. Then discuss the points that arise and look at the written transcript.

Exercise

Agree or disagree with these statements by saying 'Yes' or 'No'.
1. Mrs Cook was teaching in an infants school.
2. She happily made the children start their dinners.
3. The little girl was from the infants school.
4. The teacher threatened to punish the child if she didn't eat her dinner.
5. The little girl was fed every time she opened her mouth.
6. This experience made Mrs Cook spill her dinner.
7. The little girl will always remember that meal.

Discussion Points

a) What did you think of school food? Why do people in colleges, hospitals, and so on, often grumble about the food?
b) Do you approve of the teacher in this story? Should children be made to eat if they don't want to?

Topic One

c) What do you think a teacher's job consists of? Should it include office work and supervising lunches, for instance?

Unedited Transcript
Once when I was a secondary teacher and was on school dinner duty I had an experience that I shan't forget. When I had started the dinners, happily I could eat mine in a smaller dining-room which was for the infants school. Usually the infants had had their dinner and gone out to play but when I went to have my dinner this day I found a little girl sitting there looking very unhappy and, standing above her, a teacher looking rather angry. After a while I gathered that the little girl wouldn't eat her dinner and the teacher said that she must. Gradually the teacher got angrier and angrier and she said that the little child would not leave the dining-room till she had eaten her dinner. Naturally this upset the little girl very much and she started to cry. As she opened her mouth to cry louder, the teacher swooped down and spooned in a mouthful of dinner. Of course this upset the child even more and she cried more and each time she opened her mouth to cry, the teacher put in another spoonful of dinner. This was a very upsetting experience for me and luckily I finished my dinner and left. I'm sure that little girl would never forget her first introduction to school food and neither will I.

Written Work
Write briefly on one of the following topics.
1. My first day at school.
2. 'Schooldays are the happiest days of your life.'
3. The advantages of the educational system in my country.
4. Priorities in education.
5. 'Those who can, do; those who can't, teach.'
6. Teaching is an art, not a science.
7. A conversation between teacher and student about an approaching exam.
8. A letter to a college in England enquiring about possible courses you might follow.
9. A short story with the moral that failure at school does not mean failure in later life.
10. A prospectus describing the school you went to, for the benefit of parents who want to send their children there.

TOPIC TWO
HOLIDAYS

Background Texts

Extracts from Holiday Brochures

Majorca with Pontinental
This idyllic spot is situated on a bay on the north-east corner of the island, overlooking a vast beach of fine sand. The surrounding countryside is hilly, with giant rocks, sand dunes, and rich-scented pine trees giving shade on the hottest days. All the simple requirements of a perfect holiday are to be found at the Cale Mesquila. Hot sun . . . sea breeze, golden sands, comfortable chalets and homely food – all the ingredients to give you an atmosphere of good fellowship, humour and romance.

Hotel Yris, Norway (Thomson Skytours)
Five minutes walk from the village centre, the Yris has lovely views of the valley and mountains. It's a spacious, extremely comfortable hotel and Mr Blindheim, the manager, and his wife, make sure the hotel lives up to its motto of 'A Home Away From Home'! The lounges (one has a small library with English books) and the attractive dining-room look on to green fields and mountain peaks. The Yris has an outdoor heated pool, a ballroom and bar, and a games room.

Cities of the Danube Cruise (Clarksons)
These are the cities and towns of Eastern Europe you thought you'd never see.
  Now, Clarksons takes you there, on a unique Danube cruise. You'll visit some of Eastern Europe's noblest cities, most fascinating countries. Explore Renaissance palaces or medieval fortresses. Cruise through the spectacular forests and peaks of the Carpathian mountains. Wander in ancient ruins or see deserted palaces. Share wine and the songs and dances of Balkan folklore with friendly locals ashore, new friends aboard.

Topic Two

Holiday Facts
i) In 1973 eight and a quarter million British tourists went overseas, 35 per cent of these went to Spain, 11 per cent to France, and 8 per cent to Italy.
ii) In 1971 there were 6,253,000 overseas visitors to England; 1,907,000 came from the U.S.A., 710,000 from France, and 698,000 from Germany.
iii) In 1973 it was estimated that there were about 200 million international tourists and that the money they spent came to around 7 per cent of world trade.

Points to Consider
a) How popular is your country for tourists? What nationalities come most often?
b) If you were trying to attract visitors to your area what attractions would you mention? Scenery, history, hospitality, weather . . .
c) What are the benefits of international tourism for the tourist and for the places they visit? Should it be encouraged?

Dialogue 1 *Holidays and Escape*
Listen to this conversation between two friends; then repeat it in small sections and discuss the points that arise.

MICHAEL: I wish people wouldn't go on about their holidays so much. All they talk about is where they went last year and where they're going next year.
TREVOR: Well why shouldn't they?
MICHAEL: Because they're living more and more in a dream world.
TREVOR: What do you mean?
MICHAEL: Well they're not really interested in their jobs so they spend all their time thinking about the two or three weeks they have off.
TREVOR: I still don't see what's wrong with that.
MICHAEL: Well I do. People should live life as it is.
TREVOR: You're taking it a bit seriously, aren't you? Holidays are only relaxation.
MICHAEL: But they could be so much more – education, culture, the chance to meet different people . . . In spite of all our dashing around, we don't know each other any better.
TREVOR: I suppose there's something in that but you'll never stop people using their holidays just to escape their troubles.

Holidays

Talking Points
a) What kind of things do holiday resorts offer that you can't get at home? How valuable are they?
b) Why are holidays so important to many people? Is it just escapism?
c) What benefits could come from tourism other than simply sight-seeing? What benefits have you experienced yourself?

Dialogue 2 *Back from Holiday*
First read this conversation between three business colleagues silently. Then choose parts and read the conversation aloud. Finally discuss any points that arise.

PHILIP: Had a good holiday?
LORRAINE: All right, thank you. We went to Spain actually.
PHILIP: Oh? What was it like?
LORRAINE: We enjoyed ourselves very much. The weather was fine and we just lay on the beach all day. It felt really marvellous being thoroughly lazy for a change.
PHILIP: Well you're certainly looking brown. *We* went touring round Scotland.
LORRAINE: What was the weather like there?
PHILIP: Not as hot as Spain, I suppose, but pretty good. Fascinating country. I'd never realised how beautiful it was.
LORRAINE: Yes, I've always wanted to go there. What about you, John? Where did *you* go?
JOHN: Oh I stayed at home and mowed the lawn.
PHILIP: That doesn't sound much of a holiday.
JOHN: Well with two small children, it's a bit of a problem going away. Hotels are impossible and even camping's difficult. So we decided to stay at home and just go out for the day.
LORRAINE: That sounds sensible.
JOHN: It's surprising how little one knows of one's own country. Do you know I'd never been to the Tower of London before?

Talking Points
a) Which of these holidays would you have preferred and why?
b) How important is the weather to a holiday? What can you do on holiday if it rains all the time?
c) What are the advantages of foreign travel compared with travel in your own country?

Topic Two

Activity 1 *Holiday Questionnaire*
Tick the answers that you agree with most.
1. The best reason for choosing a place to go for your holiday is
a) the weather.
b) the sports available.
c) the entertainment available in the evenings.
d) the local people.
e) the scenery.
f) the local food and drink.
g) none of these.
2. When you travel more than 300 kilometres do you prefer to go
a) by car?
b) by train?
c) by plane?
d) by boat?
e) none of these?
3. What attracts you most about air travel?
a) the swiftness
b) the food
c) the comfort
d) the air-hostesses
4. Which of these countries would you most like to visit on holiday?
a) Switzerland
b) Kenya
c) China
d) Peru
e) Sweden
f) Hawaii
5. Which would you prefer?
a) a long summer holiday only
b) a short winter holiday and a short summer holiday
c) a long winter holiday only
d) two short holidays when you feel like it
6. Do you usually spend your holidays
a) as a sightseer in your own country?
b) as a sightseer in a foreign country?
c) doing something active in your own country?
d) doing something active in a foreign country?
7. What is the most important feature of a hotel?
a) the price
b) the friendliness of the staff

c) the food
  d) the entertainment available
8. Camping is suitable for
  a) those who are tough.
  b) those who are poor.
  c) those who have small children.
  d) anyone.
9. Which of these reasons for tourism is most important?
  a) meeting and understanding new people
  b) relaxing in a pleasant climate
  c) bringing money to poorer countries
  d) seeing beautiful scenery and historic places
10. How much paid holiday should people be entitled to every year?
  a) one week
  b) two weeks
  c) three weeks
  d) more than three weeks

Activity 2 *Silford Travel*

Silford Travel Agency have organised a coach tour of Europe, on which the following people are going:

Peter Griffin, the courier in charge of the party. He is a student studying languages at Sussex University; he works on coach tours in his holidays to earn money and to practice his languages.

Alf Higgins, the coach driver. He comes from the East End of London and has spent his life driving coaches and lorries. He doesn't particularly mind where he is, so long as the beer is all right.

Jane Green, a secretary who works in a small office in the City of London. She is about twenty, is quite pretty, and has never been abroad before.

Mrs Flaherty, an old lady. She wears thick black clothes whatever the weather and talks all the time about her dog, which she had to leave at home. She is rude to almost everyone except the courier.

Mr and Mrs Erroll. Both in their thirties, he is an accountant, she a housewife. They appear wealthy and do not speak very much to the other passengers.

25

Topic Two

The Courier's Problems

Peter Griffin has to deal with the following problems on the tour. How do you suggest he should handle them?

i) In Paris Mrs Erroll complains of pains in her stomach because of the foreign food, she says. The doctor cannot decide how serious the illness is and whether she should be allowed to travel.

ii) In Geneva Alf drinks too much beer at lunch. The coach is due to leave to drive over the Alps to Italy.

iii) In Venice, Jane Green falls in love with the waiter at the hotel. Peter knows that this waiter chases one girl on every tour; is it part of his job to warn her?

iv) In Rome Mr Erroll claims that his wallet containing his passport and money was stolen from his hotel room. There was a large notice in the room asking guests to leave valuables with the receptionist.

v) In Vienna they discover the hotel they were going to stay at has burnt down to the ground.

vi) In Zurich the other passengers complain that Mrs Flaherty is ruining their holiday by being so unpleasant.

Situations

Take the parts of the different characters and act out the following situations.

i) Peter Griffiths is showing them round a museum in Paris. He describes the paintings they see and the passengers react in different ways.

ii) The passengers discuss whether they should give Alf a tip at the end of the tour.

iii) The Customs in England have been warned that one of the people on the coach is smuggling watches. Two students play Customs Officers. The character who is the smuggler is decided by taking six pieces of paper, putting a cross on one and then folding them up. The pieces are given out and the person who receives the cross is the smuggler; of course nobody else must know this. The Customs Officers interview the characters one by one and then decide who is the smuggler.

Activity 3 *Packing*

You are packing for your camping holiday. Check what you will need on the list.

Holidays

sun-tan lotion	books	a tent
matches	a lounge suit	sunglasses
shorts	salt	a swimming-costume
evening dress	wine	a fur coat
cards	slippers	a bucket and spade
a dressing-gown	a television set	high-heeled boots
a raincoat	strawberries	thick pullovers
an iron	a saucepan	a stove

What else has been forgotten?

Activity 4 *Photographs*

Photo 1   *Blackpool Beach*
Describe what the people are doing. Do you think this is an attractive scene? Would you like a holiday like this?

1

Topic Two

2

3

Holidays

Photo 2 *Loch Ech, Scotland*
Describe the scene and what the man is doing. What kind of person goes on fishing holidays? Compare this type of holiday with the one shown in Photo 1.

Photo 3 *Buckingham Palace*
Describe the scene and the people. What other tourist attractions have you heard of in England? What are the most celebrated ones in your area?

Activity 5 *Short Talks*
Prepare and give a short talk lasting two to three minutes on one of the following topics.
1. The best holiday I have ever had.
2. Where to spend your holidays.
3. Holidays and weather.
4. A day by the sea.
5. Sporting holidays.
6. The best way to get to know a place.
7. A visit to a historic building.
8. The joys of camping.
9. My favourite kind of holiday.
10. The worst hotel I've ever stayed in.

Listening Passage 1 *An Interview*
Listen to this interview between a television reporter and Mr and Mrs Erroll, two people just returning from holiday. Then look at the questions. Listen to the interview again as many times as you need to answer the questions. Finally discuss any points that arise and look at the written text.

Questions
Tick the answer that fits the passage best.
1. a) Both the Errolls want to go on a coach tour again.
   b) Both the Errolls had wanted to go on a coach tour.
   c) Only Mr Erroll had wanted to go on a coach tour.
2. The coach was a) fit.
   b) worn out.
   c) kept in a museum.
3. Mrs Erroll thinks the hotels were all
   a) terrible.
   b) full of ghosts.
   c) burnt out.

Topic Two

4. Mrs Erroll claims that
a) someone stole Mr Erroll's wallet.
b) Mr Erroll told someone to steal his wallet.
c) Mr Erroll stole someone's wallet.
5. Mr Erroll is going to get his money back from
a) the police.
b) his solicitor.
c) the travel agents.

Discussion Points
a) Do you think their coach tour was as bad as they make out? What would you expect from a coach tour?
b) What can you do when your holiday goes wrong? Or is it simply bad luck?
c) How would you manage if you lost your money and passport in a country where you couldn't speak the language?

Written Text
INTERVIEWER: I'm from Silford Television and we're interviewing people for a programme on holidays we're showing next month. What kind of holiday have *you* had?
MR ERROLL: Terrible. Quite, quite terrible. We certainly won't go on a coach tour again.
MRS ERROLL: Well I didn't want to go by coach in the first place.
INTERVIEWER: What exactly was the matter?
MR ERROLL: The coach itself for a start. It was so old and battered the only place it was fit for was a museum.
INTERVIEWER: I see.
MRS ERROLL: But it was those third-rate hotels they put us up in that was worst. One night we even had to drive around for three hours to find the hotel.
MR ERROLL: Well the right hotel had burnt down, dear.
MRS ERROLL: And then my husband had his wallet stolen. The fuss they made was quite incredible. And the police were most unhelpful; they actually said it was his fault.
INTERVIEWER: So you're not pleased with your holiday?
MR ERROLL: You're telling me I'm not! The first thing I do when we get home is ring up my solicitor and try to get our money back.
MRS ERROLL: Not that the money matters to us.
MR ERROLL: No. It's the principle of the thing.

Holidays

Listening *Staying in Hotels*
Passage 2 This passage is an extract from a live conversation about holidays in which there are three speakers: Darryl Whiteley and Peter Burch, both lecturers in German, and Vivian Cook, a lecturer in linguistics. They are discussing some of the disadvantages of staying in English hotels, particularly the kinds of rules and regulations that English hotels often impose.
   Listen to the conversation at least once before looking at the exercise. Listen to the talk again as many times as you need. Then discuss the points that arise and look at the written transcript. This has two versions; an unedited version, which is what the speakers actually said, and an edited version.

Exercise
Agree or disagree with these statements by saying 'Yes' or 'No'.
1. The first speaker, Darryl Whiteley, was excited when he first stayed in hotels.
2. He thinks expensive hotels may be better than smaller ones.
3. The second speaker, Vivian Cook, thinks that English landladies are improving.
4. The third speaker, Peter Burch, agrees with him.
5. He thinks that big hotels have less rules and restrictions than small ones.
6. Darryl Whiteley sympathizes with the hotel's problems to some extent.
7. He often likes to eat in mid-afternoon.

Discussion Points
a) What kind of restrictions do you think hotels should put on their guests' behaviour? How much restriction would you put up with as a guest?
b) Are hotels in your country more tolerant than they are in England? Have they changed in recent years?
c) Should hotels and restaurants serve meals only at certain times, as they usually do in England, or should they remain open most of the time?

Unedited Transcript
DARRYL WHITELEY: After the the initial thrill of being able to afford to stay in a hotel wore off, I found them terrible places. I mean perhaps if one can afford a sufficiently expensive one, it's not like that but er these sort of smaller hotels where it's

31

Topic Two

like a private house but it's not your private house and you can't behave as you would at home.

VIVIAN COOK: Surely that's dying out in England now? You don't get quite these dragons of landladies telling you when you have to do things and little notices up – you know, 'Don't do this: do do that.'

PETER BURCH: Oh yes you do.

VIVIAN COOK: Do you? I mean . . .

PETER BURCH: London is absolutely full of them – small private hotels, and you're supposed to be in at a particular time at night, let's say half past eleven, and breakfast will be served between half past seven and half past eight and if you come downstairs too late, that's it. And the same applies in big hotels very often as well in this country.

DARRYL WHITELEY: Yes, particularly the meals. I think that um I mean you can understand, from the hotel's point of view, they've got to got to have a fairly restricted period when they serve meals and you're supposed to announce in advance if you want dinner and that kind of thing but I don't know about three o'clock in the afternoon whether I want to eat and, if I do want to eat, whether I want to eat at six-thirty to seven-thirty that evening. You know even if they give you an hour to start your meal, it's it's not enough.

Edited Transcript

DARRYL WHITELEY: After the initial thrill of staying in a hotel wore off, I found them terrible places. Perhaps it's not like that in an expensive one. In smaller hotels it's like a private house but it's not *your* private house and you can't behave as you would at home.

VIVIAN COOK: Surely that's dying out in England now? You don't find dragons of landladies who tell you when you have to do things and put up little notices about what you must and mustn't do.

PETER BURCH: Yes, you do. London is full of small private hotels where you're supposed to be in at a particular time at night, and breakfast is served between half past seven and half past eight; if you come down too late, you miss it. And the same is often true of big hotels as well in this country.

DARRYL WHITELEY: Yes, the mealtimes are the worst. I can understand why, from the hotel's point of view, they have to have a restricted period when they serve meals and it's convenient if the guests announce in advance whether they

Holidays

want dinner. However, I don't know at three o'clock in the afternoon whether I want to eat in the hotel, or whether, if I do, I want to eat at six-thirty to seven-thirty. Even if they give you an hour to start your meal, it's not enough.

Written Work
Write briefly on one of the following topics.
1. A famous tourist attraction.
2. The purposes of holidays.
3. The holiday that went wrong.
4. 'A change is as good as a rest.'
5. Holidays and escapism.
6. The right to have a paid holiday.
7. The tourist industry – fairy godmother or wicked stepmother?
8. A brochure advertising a holiday you would like to go on.
9. A letter to a travel agent making arrangements for your holiday in England.
10. A conversation between a tourist and a local inhabitant.

TOPIC THREE
THE SUPERNATURAL

Background Text

Varieties of the Supernatural

In one way or another most people talk about the supernatural. In its most common form this is simply a matter of superstition: what actions do we think are lucky or unlucky? In England for instance it is lucky for a black cat to cross your path; it is unlucky to walk under a ladder or break a mirror; it is lucky to find a four-leaved clover; it is unlucky to spill salt.

A more serious form of the supernatural is the poltergeist – an invisible being that is supposed to throw objects and furniture around. Strangely enough most poltergeists have manifested themselves when a young child is living in the house; some people say that this shows that the child is faking the phenomena, others that the child acts as a kind of channel for psychic energy.

Even scientists have paid some attention to the supernatural. Several have investigated different aspects of E.S.P. (Extra-Sensory Perception). Some have studied how people can transmit their thoughts by telepathy and can tell, for example, what card another person is looking at even if they are hundreds of miles away. Many experiments seem to show that there is indeed something at work; however, critics have pointed out that the results could have been achieved by cheating, for instance in some experiments by children communicating with high-pitched whistles that adults cannot hear.

Coming within the same field of speculation is the flying saucer or U.F.O. (Unidentified Flying Object). In the nineteen-fifties particularly, many people claimed to have seen mysterious flying objects in the sky like the one shown in photo 1 on page 39, sometimes large and cigar-shaped, sometimes small and round and shining with a bright light. They were seen, not just by untrained people on the ground, but by observers and pilots. One pilot is even supposed to one high in the air; what he found nobody knows xploded. At least one man claims to have a saucer, who turned out to be from

The Supernatural

the planet Venus and to be rather concerned about human beings testing nuclear bombs.

Supernatural Facts
i) The results of a public opinion poll in 1966 seem to show that about five million Americans have seen something they believe to be a U.F.O., and that about half the population think that U.F.O.s are real, not imaginary.
ii) In England Alice Mollard was the last person to be executed as a witch, as recently as 1684.

Points to Consider
a) What superstitions are there in your country? Are they the same as the ones mentioned?
b) Have you ever experienced something you thought was telepathy? How do you account for it?
c) Have you ever seen a U.F.O.? Do you think they have a natural explanation or that they are really space-ships from another planet?

Dialogue 1 *Dreams*
Listen to this conversation between two friends; then repeat it in small sections and discuss the points that arise.
JIM: I dreamed I had a car crash last night.
HELEN: Did you? You'd better be careful how you drive.
JIM: Don't be silly; that's just superstition.
HELEN: I'm not so sure. An aunt of mine once dreamed that someone was going to die and next day she had a letter from Australia to say her sister had been killed.
JIM: That doesn't prove anything. People only remember the dreams that come true and forget all the others.
HELEN: You're too cynical. What about all those people who wake up in the middle of the night feeling deathly cold and discover next day that that was the very moment when someone close to them died?
JIM: Same explanation. You only remember it when it's right and forget the ten thousand occasions when it isn't. Actually *I* woke up last week in the middle of the night feeling deathly cold.
HELEN: Don't frighten me. What happened?
JIM: Somebody had left the window open.

Topic Three

Talking Points

a) Have *you* ever had a dream that seemed to come true? What explanation is there for this?

b) Are all 'spirit messages' coincidence and the result of a selective memory? What about when several people receive the same 'message'?

c) Which do you think is the better attitude to have towards the supernatural, Jim's or Helen's?

Dialogue 2 *Visitors from Space*

First read this conversation between two friends silently. Then choose parts and read the conversation aloud. Finally discuss any points that arise.

HENRY: This book I'm reading says we're all descended from spacemen.

ROY: What?

HENRY: Well it claims that thousands of years ago spacemen came to Earth.

ROY: That sounds a bit unlikely. What's the evidence?

HENRY: Mostly the enormous ancient monuments like the Pyramids. They simply couldn't have been made by primitive methods.

ROY: I thought it was a question of using thousands of slaves.

HENRY: Even then it wouldn't work. Think of the stones at Stonehenge which were transported hundreds of miles.

ROY: I still think sheer numbers would manage it.

HENRY: But the most interesting thing is a place in South America where there are huge patterns on the ground that look exactly like animals if you fly over them.

ROY: What's special about that?

HENRY: Well it shows they could fly.

ROY: Does it! I suppose the author is one of these spacemen himself?

HENRY: Don't be silly. It's a serious book.

Talking Points

a) How seriously do you take suggestions that the Earth was visited by spacemen? How could it be proved to be true? Would it matter if it were true?

b) What strange constructions like the Pyramids in Egypt or Stonehenge in England are there in your country? Are there any legends about them?

The Supernatural

Activity 1 *Supernatural Questionnaire*
Tick the answers that you agree with most.
1. If a black cat crosses your path do you think that it is
a) lucky?
b) unlucky?
c) neither?
2. Which of the following do you regard as lucky, if any?
a) chimney-sweeps
b) horse-shoes
c) Friday 13th
d) four-leaved clovers
e) ladders
f) looking at the new moon through glass
3. When you spill some salt, do you
a) think nothing of it?
b) throw some over your left shoulder?
c) carry out some other act?
4. Which of the following people you know has seen a ghost?
a) you yourself
b) one of your family
c) one of your friends
d) someone you have met
e) someone you have heard of but not met
f) nobody
5. If you were walking along a dark road and saw a white figure cross the road and disappear through what looked like a solid wall would you
a) pay no special attention?
b) run away?
c) decide you must have been mistaken?
d) inspect the wall for a door?
e) resolve to visit your doctor?
6. Do you think E.S.P.
a) doesn't exist?
b) exists and is an unexplained physical phenomenon?
c) exists and is a religious or mystical phenomenon?
7. U.F.O.s are really
a) fakes.
b) hallucinations.
c) spaceships from another world.
d) weather balloons and other natural objects.
8. If you met a creature from another planet would you
a) welcome him?

Topic Three

    b) shoot him?
    c) pinch yourself to see if you were dreaming?
    d) shout for help?

Activity 2 *The Silford Ghost*
Last month a ghost was reported to have been seen in the town of Silford. Three of the inhabitants tell the following stories:
MRS DAWSON (*a housewife*): Well I was just coming back from a visit to my mother's – she's had the 'flu you see. It was eleven o'clock at night and very dark and wet. We were crossing the High Street when we saw a great white horse come galloping round the corner by the Town Hall. He went right past us, so close I could have put my hand out and touched him. He was shining all over. Of course we knew at once he was a ghost because his hooves didn't make any noise.
WILLIAM MUIR (*a businessman*): I'd been at the pub all evening. I hadn't had much to drink – you know, just the usual. Well I started driving home and then I saw this idiot on a white horse riding down the middle of the road. I honked and honked at him but he still wouldn't get out of the way. Then he suddenly sort of vanished; I suppose he went down a side-street or jumped over a wall or something; anyway I couldn't see him any more. People with horses shouldn't be allowed out at night, that's my opinion.
JAMES BRODIE (*a 95-year-old retired farm labourer*): Any ghosts round here? I could tell you a tale or two. There's old Sir Hubert, for instance. Many is the time I saw him when I was a lad. 'Course I'm ninety-seven now, you know. Well Sir Hubert had been away at the wars for twenty years leaving his beautiful young wife sorrowing at home. There he was on his way home at last after all these years, when just by where the Town Hall stands now, he and his horse fell into a hole and both their necks were broken. And for the last three hundred years he and his horse have been trying to get home.

A committee have been sent to investigate the Silford ghost; they try to establish what was really seen by interviewing the witnesses and any other inhabitants of Silford. Eventually they have to make a report about whether they think it was a genuine ghost. One group of students play the committee; others take the parts of the witnesses, the other inhabitants, and, if required, the ghost.

The Supernatural

Activity 3 *Photographs*

Photo 1   *A Flying Saucer*
Describe what the saucer looks like and suggest what it might be. Have you ever seen anything like this?

1

Topic Three

Photo 2   *A Faked Photo of the Ghost of W. B. Yeats*
Describe the ghost and suggest how it was faked. Do you think there are any 'real' photos of ghosts?

Photo 3   *The Ghost of Hamlet's Father*
Describe the scene. What other famous ghosts are there in literature?

The Supernatural

Activity 4 *Short Talks*
Prepare and give a short talk lasting two to three minutes on one of the following topics.
1. My lucky number.
2. Telling the future.
3. The time I saw a ghost.
4. Flying saucers have landed!
5. People who see ghosts should see doctors.
6. The time someone read my thoughts.
7. An accident avoided through a dream.
8. The best magic trick I have ever seen.
9. Why people like ghost stories.
10. Science and the supernatural.

Listening Passage 1 *The Red Indian Curse*
Listen to this story about a water diviner's adventure in Canada. Then look at the questions. Listen to the story again as many times as you like. Finally discuss any points that arise and look at the written text.

Questions
Tick the answer that fits the passage best.
1. A water diviner looks for water
a) with scientific instruments.
b) alone.
c) with a twig.
2. Before she could start divining she
a) had to
b) didn't have to
c) wasn't able to
visit the area.
3. The gold-mine she visited was
a) cleared out.
b) in an open space.
c) Red Indian.
4. She believed the mine would be unsuccessful because the Red Indians
a) had put a magic spell on it.
b) had taken all the gold.
c) would try to prevent it.
5. The miners decided to give up looking because
a) Miss Penrose warned them.
b) the Red Indians had threatened them.
c) several accidents happened.

41

Topic Three

Discussion Points
a) Do you believe in water divining? What explanation is there for its successes?
b) Do you think that some places have curses on them? What examples of primitive magic that seems to work have you heard of?
c) Why is gold mining often the subject of adventure stories and coal mining never? What other jobs are romantic and dangerous at the same time?

Written Text
A water diviner usually locates underground water solely with a twig in his hands rather than with scientific instruments. One of the most famous diviners was Evelyn Penrose who led a highly adventurous life, looking, not just for water, but for diamonds in South Africa, oil in California, and coal in England; sometimes she would even work by looking at a map of the area without visiting it. Once when she was the official Government water diviner in British Columbia, she was asked to divine gold. It was a long hard journey to the mine which was in a clearing in the dense forest. When she reached it, she became more and more uneasy without knowing any reason. Then she realised that the Red Indians must have put a curse on the place to bring harm to any other people who went there. At first the miners didn't believe her when she told them. Then she and an old miner were dangerously lost for hours in the forest; one miner lost two fingers in a machine, another broke his leg; finally the mine tunnel collapsed and seriously injured two more miners and they decided they had had enough. However Miss Penrose became seriously ill and it was many weeks before she recovered from the effects of the curse.

Listening *Ghosts*
Passage 2 This is an extract from a live conversation about ghosts between two main speakers, Miss Jenny Drew and Mrs Jennifer Bagg. Both of them are students studying English at a polytechnic in London. Jenny Drew tells a story about her family ghosts and they discuss how frightened they would be if they really saw one.
    Listen to the conversation and then look at the exercise. As you listen to it again try to do the exercise. Listen to it again as many times as you need. Then discuss the points that arise

The Supernatural

and look at the written transcript: there are two versions of this, edited and unedited.

Exercise
Agree or disagree with these statements by saying 'Yes' or 'No'.
1. The first speaker, Jenny Drew, mentions two ghosts in her family.
2. She says that her great grandmother's ghost was seen by only one person.
3. She says that her grandmother saw the ghost.
4. The second speaker, Mrs Bagg, is amazed at this story.
5. She thinks that she would be frightened by a ghost.
6. She implies that you can tell a ghost by trying to touch it.

Discussion Points
a) Are some families particularly sensitive to the supernatural? In what ways?
b) How much would you be frightened by a ghost?
c) What methods are there for telling if something is a ghost?

Unedited Transcript
JENNY DREW: My uncle and my grandmother – no, my uncle and my grandfather both saw my grandfather's mother after she'd died and my sister keeps seeing my grandfather.
MRS BAGG: At the same time do they see the ghost?
JENNY DREW: Well it was the it was the same night. Um my uncle said 'You know, Granny came back last night. I saw her standing at the end of my bed.' My grandmother said 'Rubbish.'
MRS BAGG: Yeah.
JENNY DREW: My grandfather said 'No, she was standing at the end of our bed as well.'
MRS BAGG: Oh, how extraordinary.
JENNY DREW: So ... Yes 'cos, 'cos quite a lot of things like that.
MRS BAGG: I mean, were they frightened? 'Cos I think if I actually ...
JENNY DREW: No.
MRS BAGG: ... saw a ghost, because I don't believe in them really, I would be frightened, you know, to think that I was completely wrong.
JENNY DREW: You probably wouldn't ...
VIVIAN COOK: More so than ...

43

Topic Three

MRS BAGG: More so than if I did, I was expecting it.
JENNY DREW: No, I don't think they were frightened; I think I would be probably.
MRS BAGG: I'd want to touch it and see if it was real and if you put your hand through it, you'd know that it was a ghost.

Edited Transcript
JENNY DREW: My uncle and my grandfather both saw my great-grandmother after she'd died and my sister keeps seeing my grandfather.
MRS BAGG: Did they see the ghost at the same time?
JENNY DREW: Well it was the same night. My uncle said next day that he'd seen his grandmother standing at the foot of his bed. My grandmother said 'Rubbish'.
MRS BAGG: Yeah.
JENNY DREW: But my grandfather said that she was standing at the foot of *their* bed as well.
MRS BAGG: How extraordinary. Were they frightened?
JENNY DREW: No, I don't think they were frightened.
MRS BAGG: If I actually saw a ghost, I'd be frightened because I don't believe in them. More so than if I was expecting it.
JENNY DREW: I think I'd be frightened.
MRS BAGG: I'd want to touch it and see if it was real. If you could put your hand through it, you'd know it was a ghost.

Written Work
Write briefly on one of the following topics.
1. Luck or Fate?
2. The dangers of investigating the supernatural.
3. Telepathy is only a matter of waves, like radio.
4. A haunted house.
5. Dreams and reality.
6. Miracles.
7. The supernatural and religion.
8. Why some people fake supernatural phenomena.
9. A conversation between a husband and wife in the middle of the night about a noise downstairs that has woken them up.
10. A letter to a friend describing a horror film you have seen or a ghost story you have read.

TOPIC FOUR
HOUSES

Background Text *Housing in Britain*

In the past few years housing in Britain has been a problem with many aspects. One is the supply of houses. Due to the expanding population, to the low rate of building new houses, and to the age of many existing houses, there have not been enough houses to go round. Not only have many people been homeless but also many others have been living in overcrowded buildings of a low standard. Though the government and charities such as Shelter have been trying hard to remedy this situation, there are still immense problems, particularly around the centres of the larger cities.

There are three basic forms of accommodation. In the first place some own their own house or flat; often the money for this is borrowed from a building society on a 'mortgage' and is paid back over twenty or thirty years. Secondly many people live in council flats or houses; these are owned by the local council and rented out. Council housing has aroused controversial political issues about whether council tenants should pay the full rent or should be subsidized, and whether they should have the opportunity to buy their houses if they like. Thirdly some people rent accommodation from private landlords, either furnished or unfurnished; a complicated set of laws and regulations defines the rights of landlords and tenants, governing, for instance, when landlords can force tenants to leave and how much rent they can charge.

A further problem since about 1970 has been the tremendous rise in the price of housing. In the London area the value of houses doubled in about two years; although prices have levelled off, they are unlikely to return to their earlier levels. People who already own houses have not been too badly affected, since the rise in the value of the house they are selling to some extent cancels out the rise in the price of a house they wish to move to. However, it has made house-buying extremely difficult for those who are buying a house for the first time, such as young married couples.

Topic Four

Facts about Housing in 1971
i) 31 per cent of households in Great Britain lived in buildings constructed before 1919, 27 per cent in buildings constructed between 1919 and 1944, and 42 per cent in buildings constructed after 1945.
ii) 9 per cent of households had no bath, 10 per cent no indoor W.C., 1 per cent no W.C. at all.
iii) 22 per cent of households owned their own accommodation outright, 27 per cent owned them with a mortgage, 31 per cent rented them from local councils, 14 per cent rented them privately.

Points to Consider
a) Are the housing problems in your country similar to those in England or quite different? In what ways?
b) Should every house have a bath? What proportion of houses in your country don't have amenities such as baths?
c) Are the ages of property similar in your country? The system of ownership similar or quite different?

Dialogue 1 *Buying a House*
Listen to this conversation between two colleagues; then repeat it in small sections and discuss the points that arise.
SUSAN: Did I tell you we'd found a house at last?
TOM: Have you? I thought you'd given up looking.
SUSAN: Well we had really but Bill just happened to drive past one on his way to work that had a sign up.
TOM: That was lucky. What's it like?
SUSAN: It's a terrace actually. One of those enormous Victorian houses built for Victorian families, terribly ugly outside but lovely and roomy inside.
TOM: Yes that kind of house is all right if it's in good condition.
SUSAN: It doesn't look too bad. All the major things are all right – the roof doesn't leak, the walls aren't damp. It really only needs redecorating.
TOM: That shouldn't be too expensive.
SUSAN: No, Bill's quite good at it once he gets going.
TOM: How about the mortgage?
SUSAN: Well the building society seem prepared to lend us all we're asking for.
TOM: That's a change.

Houses

Talking Points
a) What kind of house would you like to live in?
b) What kinds of things would you look for when buying a house? What kinds of things should you be careful about?
c) Do you think people should redecorate their own houses or should they hire professionals?

Dialogue 2 *New Furniture*
First read this conversation between husband and wife silently. Then choose parts and read the conversation aloud. Finally discuss any points that arise.
MARK: I'm getting fed up with these chairs.
ROSEMARY: But we've had them since we got married.
MARK: That doesn't mean we've got to have them the rest of our lives. Anyway they're falling apart.
ROSEMARY: But they're so comfortable. I don't fancy any of those shiny new ones.
MARK: I didn't say we'd have shiny chairs or uncomfortable ones. In fact I saw a rather nice suite in Habitat last week.
ROSEMARY: Well new chairs would mean changing the curtains. And the carpet as well. Think what it would cost.
MARK: We could buy a colour that matched what we already have.
ROSEMARY: Oh no. If we're going to have new chairs, I don't want imitations of the old ones. We might as well do things properly.
MARK: You may be right.
ROSEMARY: And if we moved the old chairs into the children's room, we could get rid of their old stuff.
MARK: Oh.
ROSEMARY: And then we could start on the kitchen.
MARK: All right, all right, all right, you've made your point. I'll forget about the chairs.

Talking Points
a) How long should furniture last? Should one change it because one is tired of it or because it's old?
b) How does Rosemary persuade Mark not to get new chairs? Is this a fair trick?
c) What furniture is essential and functional, what is luxurious and optional?

Topic Four

Activity 1 *Housing Questionnaire*
Tick the answers that you agree with most.
1. Which would you prefer to live in?
a) a new flat
b) a two-hundred-year-old house
c) a new house
d) a bungalow
e) a caravan
2. Would you rather live in
a) the centre of a city?
b) the suburbs of a city?
c) a small town?
d) a village?
e) a completely isolated spot?
3. When people are first married should they
a) live with the husband's or wife's mother?
b) live near the husband's or wife's mother?
c) live as far as possible away from their relations?
d) none of these?
4. The most important thing in choosing a house is
a) the price.
b) the area.
c) the size.
d) a combination of these.
e) none of these.
5) Do you think that people's accommodation should belong to
a) the State or local council?
b) themselves?
c) a private landlord?
d) a cooperative or commune?
6. Which of these noises irritates you most?
a) traffic
b) planes
c) children
d) factories
e) dogs
f) amplified music from radios and so on
7. In developing a town centre, which of the following aims would you consider most important?
a) attractive new buildings
b) more open space
c) more facilities for entertainment/leisure
d) traffic-free shopping streets

Houses

e) more convenient bus services
f) new housing development
8. Do you think that conserving the natural features of the country is
a) more important than providing houses for everyone?
b) less important than providing houses for everyone?
c) of no particular importance?

Activity 2 *Silford Town Centre*
The town of Silford has had severe traffic problems for many years not only because it is an important industrial town but also because several important roads pass through it. The town centre is made up of historic buildings of great beauty and architectural importance; the area immediately surrounding the centre contains parks, meadows and other open spaces; the outer suburbs consists either of terrace houses or of factories.
  Three plans have been suggested to solve this problem.
  1. The Northern By-pass. This would involve building a by-pass to take heavy traffic through the outer suburbs; it would mean knocking down 347 houses and closing 3 factories.
  2. The Inner By-pass. This would run across the river meadows, North Park, and Victoria Park; it would mean knocking down 27 houses and losing most of the open spaces in the town.
  3. The Central Relief Plan. This would improve the existing roads through the centre by widening, by one-way systems, by traffic lights, and so on.
The Government have sent a committee of inquiry to decide between these plans: one group of students play the committee. The remaining students have to give evidence to the committee. One group represent a residents association from the outer suburbs who dislike plan 1 because it will destroy houses and employment. Another group are 'conservationists' who dislike plan 2 because it will destroy the green open spaces. A third group are shopkeepers and residents of the town centre who are against plan 3 because it will destroy the character of the town. The three groups decide among themselves what arguments to use and then present their evidence. Any other inhabitants who wish to give evidence can, of course, do so. Finally the committee has to give a decision.

Topic Four

The Town of Silford. Population: 129,000. Industries: car manufacturing, blankets, tourists. Ancient monuments: Cathedral of St. John, St. Barnabas College.

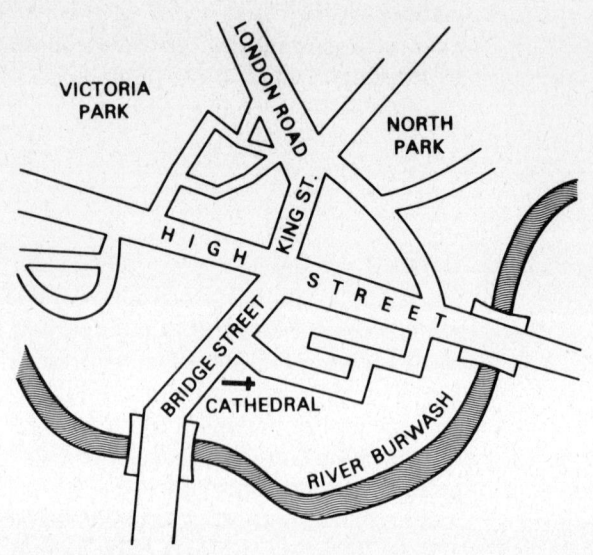

Activity 3 *Furnishing a Flat*

You are moving into a flat with the floor plan given below. Decide where you will put the furniture and mark the places with the appropriate numbers.

1) a television set, 2) a double bed, 3) a cooker, 4) a desk, 5) two low bookcases, 6) two upright chairs, 7) two wardrobes, 8) a settee, 9) a fridge, 10) an armchair, 11) a dressing table, 12) a chest of drawers.

What other furniture will you need to buy?

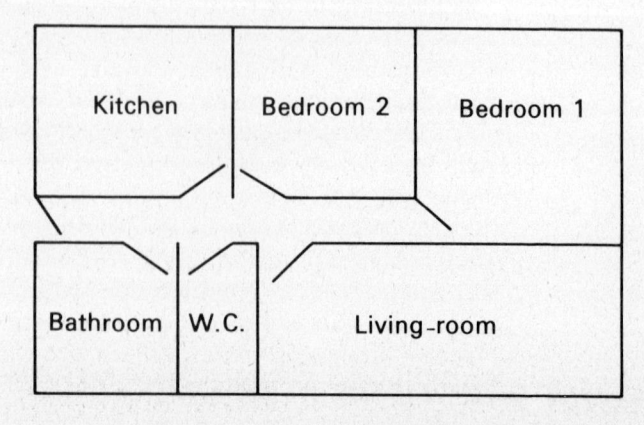

Houses

Activity 4 *Photographs*

    Photo 1   *A Modern Block*
    Describe the building. How would you like to live or work in a block like this?

1

Topic Four

2

3

Houses

Photo 2   *An Exotic Room*
Describe the room. Would you say this was a room for show or to live in?

Photo 3   *A Crowded Street*
Describe the street scene and what the people are doing. Would you rather live here or in a block like that in Photo 1?

Activity 5   *Short Talks*
Prepare and give a short talk lasting two to three minutes on one of the following topics.
1. My ideal house.
2. The pleasures of decorating your own home.
3. The advantages of flats.
4. Why should one move house?
5. The house where I'm living at the moment.
6. Colour schemes for rooms.
7. Why I live in the town/country.
8. An historic building.
9. Homes before Roads!
10. Should furniture be functional or beautiful?

Listening Passage 1   *Hampton Court*
Listen to this talk about the palace of Hampton Court. Then look at the questions. Listen to the story again as many times as you like and answer the questions. Finally discuss any points that arise and look at the written text.

Questions
Tick the answer that fits the passage best.
1. Hampton Court is on the Thames
a) in London.
b) above London.
c) below London.
2. Hampton Court was given to
a) Henry VIII.
b) Cardinal Wolsey.
c) Elizabeth I.
3. Elizabeth I was at Hampton Court when she
a) executed Mary Queen of Scots.
b) gave orders to have Mary executed.
c) already had had Mary executed.
4. Sir Christopher Wren was famous for

Topic Four

      a) mathematical knowledge.
      b) celebrating.
      c) building churches and houses.
   5. Since the time of George III the Royal Family have lived
      a) at Windsor.
      b) at Hampton Court.
      c) in a country house.

Discussion Points
a) What do you think of Henry VIII?
b) What buildings like Hampton Court do you have in your country? Should such buildings be preserved?
c) Have you ever been lost in a maze? Why are they popular?

Written Text
One of the most famous and historic buildings in England is the former Royal Palace of Hampton Court situated a few miles inland from London on the River Thames. Originally Cardinal Wolsey had the first building constructed in the reign of Henry VIII, intending to demonstrate his power and riches by the splendour of the architecture; he even had fresh water brought by pipe from Kingston Hill the other side of the river. So successful was his creation that the King is supposed to have become jealous; Wolsey felt that it would be tactful to give it to him as a present. It then became a country home for the kings and queens of England and played a part in many historic events: Elizabeth I was staying there when she decided to have Mary Queen of Scots executed; William Shakespeare is said to have performed there as an actor. A hundred years or so later, Sir Christopher Wren, the most celebrated of English architects, made considerable additions to the palace. But when George III came to the throne, he moved the country home of the Royal Family to Windsor Castle leaving Hampton Court largely to the tourists, who visit it in summer in great numbers, particularly to see its maze.

Listening Passage 2   *The Problems of Buying a House*
This is an extract from a live conversation about buying houses. The speaker, Robin Graham Bell, is an editor and writer. He describes the difficulties of buying a house in England, particularly the long delays that occur even after a price has been agreed.

Houses

Listen to the conversation and then look at the exercise. Listen to the conversation again as many times as you need to do the exercise. Then discuss the points that arise and look at the written transcript.

Exercise
Agree or disagree with these statements by saying 'Yes' or 'No'.
1. Robin Bell heard of the house through a newspaper.
2. It took him a long time to settle the price.
3. He paid for the house immediately.
4. It has taken him two weeks to finish the deal.
5. The delays have been caused by the lawyers.
6. He thinks lawyers would make successful bakers.
7. He thinks that people who sell houses run complicated companies.

Discussion Points
a) How do you set about looking for a house?
b) Does house-buying take such a long time in your country? How long should it take?
c) Are lawyers justified in the time they seem to take over what seem to be simple matters?

Unedited Transcript
I found that the process of buying a house in England is ten times more elaborate than I had thought it was. Um I'd, we saw a house advertised, went along, looked at the house, thought 'Yes, this'll suit us'. We talked to the people who own it and um really very quickly it worked out sort of an agreeable price; both we, the buyers, and they, the sellers, were satisfied. Good. You'd think that you could then exchange money and be all set. Oh no, you have to call in the lawyers and surveyors and um all kinds of other other people and this means delays in time, a great proliferation of paperwork. And in fact we first saw this house and agreed on the price almost two months ago and with any luck in about two weeks we'll know whether or not we've been able to get it. Now we've agreed on the price; the you know the seller the sellers have said 'Yes, we accept your offer'. Fine. But now our lawyers and their lawyers are wrangling over precisely how this acceptance should be phrased. And I'm afraid that um if you let lawyers get their hands on a sale of say a loaf of bread, the bread would be stale and mouldy before it could ever be sold. But no, obvi-

ously um that's not a very good analogy because buying a house selling a house is really quite a complicated business.

Written Work
Write briefly on one of the following topics.
1. The home of the future.
2. The place where I was born.
3. Buying or renting?
4. A celebrated house.
5. Conservation v. progress in housing.
6. The house is a machine for living.
7. A short advertisement to sell the house where you are living.
8. The relationship of the forms of transport to the styles of housing.
9. A conversation between an estate agent and a lady who is looking round a house.
10. Housing problems and their solution.

TOPIC FIVE
FOOD

Background Text

Recipes
These were both supplied by foreign students. The quantities given are for 6–8 people and should be adapted to suit the number required.

Norwegian Får-i-kål
INGREDIENTS   2 kilos breast of lamb. 2 kilos cabbage. Black peppercorns, salt and flour.
DIRECTIONS   Boil the cabbage in water till cooked. Cut the lamb into pieces and dip them in flour. Drain the water from the cabbage. Put a layer of meat in the bottom of a saucepan; cover it with a layer of cabbage, a layer of salt, a layer of peppercorns, a layer of meat, and so on. Pour in water till it is covered. Put a lid on the saucepan and boil gently for three hours.

French Onion Soup
INGREDIENTS   1 kilo onions. 1 bottle white wine. 1 bouquet garni (collection of assorted herbs). Gruyère cheese, French bread, oil, mustard.
DIRECTIONS   Slice the onions very thin. Melt a dessertspoonful (10 ml) of butter with two tablespoonfuls (20 ml) of cooking oil in a large frying-pan; add the onions. When the mixture is hot, let it cook slowly; then add a tablespoonful of flour and stir till it becomes sticky. Add a teaspoonful (5ml) of mustard and 1 dl of wine; stir to a smooth paste, add 1 dl water and pour into a large saucepan. Add the bouquet garni, another 1 dl water, and as much wine as you like. Simmer for 35 minutes, then taste and add any seasoning required. Prepare rounds of toasted French bread covered with grated Gruyère cheese. Put them in soup bowls and pour the soup on top.

The Vocabulary of Cooking
This is intended as an aid to following recipes in English and

Topic Five

to describing your own recipes. Some typical cooking utensils are shown in the drawing on page 63.

Methods of Preparation
SLICE: to cut into thin pieces
CHOP: to cut into large pieces
GRATE: to use a grater to cut into very small pieces
MIX: to combine several ingredients together
STIR: to rotate a spoon or egg-beater, usually in order to make smooth
BEAT: to add air by stirring vigorously
ROLL: either to flatten or to make into round shapes

Cooking Processes
BOIL: to cook vigorously in water on an open flame
SIMMER: to cook gently in water on an open flame without boiling
FRY: to cook in fat or oil
GRILL: to cook by exposing to direct heat under a flame
BAKE: to cook by dry heat in an oven
ROAST: to cook in an oven 'basting' (i.e. coating) with fat

Facts
i) In 1971 an English household with an income of £30 a week spent £8.10 on food, £1.20 on alcohol, and £1.50 on tobacco.
ii) In 1972 English people drank 2.7 litres of milk per head per week, and ate 5 eggs and 1.9 kilos of potatoes.
iii) In 1958 60 per cent of Englishmen had a cooked dish for breakfast; by 1972 this had fallen to 32 per cent.

Points to Consider
a) How does the proportion of income spent on food in England, roughly a quarter, compare with that in your country?
b) Are eating habits in your country changing as they are in England?
c) What beliefs do you have about English food? What beliefs do foreigners have about your food? Are either of them true?

Dialogue 1 *A Good Meal*
Listen to this conversation between husband and wife; then repeat it in small sections and discuss the points that arise.
ALAN: I must say I rather fancy having a good meal tonight.
BRENDA: Me too.
ALAN: Starting with avocado pears.

Food

BRENDA: Delicious but I think I'd prefer a melon. Cool and delicate. And some fresh trout to follow.
ALAN: No, I'll have veal in wine sauce.
BRENDA: Very tasty. And vegetables? How about asparagus?
ALAN: No, it'd probably be tough.
BRENDA: Don't forget the wine.
ALAN: That's a bit difficult. We'll have to see what they've got.
BRENDA: And strawberries and cream to finish with.
ALAN: That sounds wonderful. I'll go and book a table.
BRENDA: What about a baby-sitter?
ALAN: A baby-sitter? There's Mrs Jones.
BRENDA: No, she's away. There's no-one we can ask now.
ALAN: Well forget it then. What's in the fridge?
BRENDA: There's some sausages left over from last night.
ALAN: Well it's not avocado pear but it'll do.

Talking Points
a) What would your favourite meal consist of?
b) To what extent does having children limit social life?
c) Should children be left in the hands of baby-sitters while their parents go out?

Dialogue 2 *The Price of Food*
First read this conversation between three colleagues silently. Then choose parts and read the conversation aloud. Finally discuss any points that arise.
BRIAN: Do you know they're putting up the canteen prices again?
CAROL: Not again. This is ridiculous.
BRIAN: I know. They only went up last month.
CAROL: Well if I'm going to pay more I want better food than this rubbish.
JUNE: It's the cost of living, I suppose. Look at the way meat has gone up this month.
BRIAN: They say it's joining the Common Market.
CAROL: That's only an excuse.
JUNE: It's all beyond me. I only know I spend more money on food every week.
CAROL: But this canteen increase is scandalous. We only eat here because we have to.
BRIAN: We really ought to make a fuss about it this time.
JUNE: I don't suppose that would do any good.

Topic Five

Talking Points
a) Why is food getting more expensive everywhere? What can be done about it?
b) Should canteen meals make a profit or be subsidised by the employers?
c) What are the benefits, if any, of joining an organisation like the Common Market?

Activity 1 *Food Questionnaire*
Tick the answer that you agree with most.
1. Do you think people should drink alcohol
a) occasionally?
b) every day?
c) for health reasons only?
d) never?
2. The chief reason for a diet should be
a) to become healthy.
b) to become slim.
c) to save money.
d) none of these.
3. Tick which of the following you would usually eat at your main meal. (English people would usually have meat and potatoes.)
a) meat
b) potatoes
c) fish
d) rice
e) pasta (flour-based products)
f) salad
g) bread
h) curry
4. How great a proportion of a person's income should they spend on food?
a) less than 20 per cent
b) 20 to 30 per cent
c) more than 30 per cent
5. Tick any items in the following that you regard as food for humans. (Fish is the only one thought to be food in England.)
a) fish
b) snakes
c) insects (ants, locusts, etc.)
d) frogs

Food

e) dogs
f) horse
6. If a person has eaten nothing for five days, should his first meal consist of
a) bread and butter?
b) soup?
c) steak?
d) none of these?
7. If you were entertaining friends to dinner in your home which of the following would you spend most money on?
a) wine
b) meat
c) vegetables
d) none of these
8. What would you look for in a restaurant meal? Put the following in order of importance.
a) pleasant atmosphere
b) taste of the food
c) wines
d) unusualness
e) price
f) politeness of the staff

Activity 2 *Menus*

The following might be a menu for an English Sunday dinner eaten at home.

First course   Tomato soup
Main course   Roast Beef
                       Roast Potatoes
                       Peas
                       Gravy
Pudding   Apple pie

Now you must devise a menu for one of the following groups of people.
i) two ten-year-old boys
ii) your oldest friends
iii) your mother and father-in-law
iv) some foreign visitors
v) the person you are going to marry
vi) a vegetarian and a fussy old lady
vii) a girl who is slimming, a child of three, and a man
viii) a New Year's party
ix) Paul McCartney, Prince Philip, and Brigitte Bardot

Topic Five

Activity 3 *Shopping*

Although most things can now be bought at supermarkets in England, some people prefer to go to small shops. Sort out the following shopping list so that you know which shop to go to for each item.

lamb chops   apples   aspirins   writing-paper   steak
frozen peas   bananas   corn-flakes   sugar   sausages
potatoes   a magazine   cough mixture   bacon   soap
cabbage   cheese   ink   ice-cream   perfume   a pen

greengrocer's:

chemist's:

butcher's:

newsagent's:

grocer's:

Activity 4 *Situations*

Act out the following situations.
1. You have gone to your butcher's to complain that the steak he sold you yesterday was off.
2. A waitress is taking the orders of a group of people who all want different things. She leaves the room and comes back with the food which she has to give to the right people.
3. Your husband has arrived home from the office two hours late and his dinner is completely spoiled.
4. You are trying to explain to an English person how to cook the national dish of your country.
5. You are telephoning your weekly shopping list to the grocer's for him to deliver.

Activity 5 *Cookbook*

Using the recipes mentioned earlier as a model, each student has to write down their favourite recipe. The recipes are collected and turned into a class cookbook.

Food

Activity 6 *Visuals*

Cooking Utensils
Saucepan, frying-pan, kettle, rolling-pin, egg-beater, grater.

Photo 1   *Battery Hens*
Describe the hens and their cages. Do hens find it pleasant to live like this? Is it right to keep animals like this?

Topic Five

Photo 2 *A Market Stall*
Describe the stall and the people. Why would you shop in a street market?

Activity 7 *Short Talks*
Prepare and give a short talk lasting two to three minutes on one of the following topics.
1. My ideal meal.
2. What I had for breakfast this morning.
3. The food I dislike most.
4. Only greedy people talk about food.
5. Vegetarianism.
6. Food shortages.
7. Drinking alcohol is immoral.
8. Table manners.
9. The best cooks are all men.
10. Diets.

Food

Listening *My Aunt's Cooker*
Passage 1 Listen to this story about the speaker's aunt. Then look at the questions. Listen to the story again as many times as you like and answer the questions. Finally discuss any points that arise and look at the written text.

Questions
Tick the answer that fits the passage best.
1. The speaker's aunt
a) used to live in Scotland.
b) lives in Scotland now.
c) was living in Scotland at the time of the story.
2. She spent a lot of time
a) looking at television.
b) talking about television.
c) looking at scenery.
3. What she liked most was
a) a chef.
b) a washing machine.
c) a cooker.
4. In the restaurant she
a) ate hungrily.
b) talked about her cooker all the time.
c) would have preferred to eat at home.
5. When his aunt returned home she found her meal
a) hot and ready to eat.
b) cold and uncooked.
c) burned.

Discussion Points
a) How much do modern inventions contribute to cooking?
b) Are absent-minded women like his aunt common? Is this associated with men rather than women?
c) Is it a good idea for old people to move away from the place they know? For what reasons?

Written Text
My aunt had lived in a small isolated village in Scotland for most of her life. When she came to London in middle-age, she was astonished at the bustle and activity and the pace of city life. In particular she was immensely impressed by the modern inventions crammed into her tiny new flat. Hour after hour she would gaze at her colour television set, exclaiming at

Topic Five

the greenness of the grass or the blueness of the sky. Her kitchen boasted a monster of a washing machine, covered in knobs and controls and flashing lights. But best of all she loved her cooker. Undoubtedly it was a magnificent specimen. There it stood in the corner, glaring at you from behind a sort of plastic window that concealed the eye-level grill. One day she had lunch with me in a restaurant and spent the entire hour oblivious to the food, enthusing about the wonders of her cooker. She had, apparently, left her entire evening meal in the oven; at five o'clock the electric clock would start it cooking and by seven her meal would be ready to welcome her home. I almost envied her. But next time we met she told me what had actually happened: however automatic your cooker, however accurate your electric clock, you've still got to turn them on.

Listening Passage 2 *Takeaway Food*

This is an extract from a live conversation about food. The speakers are Darryl Whiteley and Peter Burch who are both lecturers in German, and Mrs Pam Cook, a housewife and ex-teacher. They are discussing eating out and in particular the phenomenon that has recently appeared in England of the 'takeaway' restaurant where you can buy hot cooked food and take it away to eat. They feel this type of restaurant reflects the unsociability of the English, also shown in their habits of not talking to strangers and not dining out in groups.

Listen to the conversation and then look at the exercise. Listen to the conversation again as many times as you need to do the exercise. Then discuss the points that arise and look at the written transcript. There are two versions of the transcript, edited and unedited.

Exercise
Agree or disagree with these statements by saying 'Yes' or 'No'.
1. The first speaker, Darryl Whiteley, thinks that pubs are increasing in popularity.
2. He says that nowadays people only go to pubs with people they know.
3. He thinks takeaways help you to meet new people.
4. The second speaker, Peter Burch, thinks that friendliness is typical of modern society.
5. Pam Cook wants to know how often Chinese people eat out.
6. She thinks that eating out is rare among English people.

7. Peter Burch agrees that it's only done on special occasions.
8. Darryl Whiteley agrees that it doesn't happen very often.

Discussion Points
a) Is it true that people are becoming less sociable? What are the reasons?
b) What national characteristics in eating-out patterns can you think of? Special occasions? Groups?
c) What ways are there of meeting new people?

Unedited Transcript
DARRYL WHITELEY: I think takeaways is all part of this er lack of sociability that's increasing all the time. Like pubs. At one time you you you would expect to go into a pub where you didn't know anybody and you'd expect there was a fair chance of getting into conversation with somebody there. Now they're all being done up and therefore places to go already for people already in closed groups: they don't mix with the other groups there, they just go in their group. I suppose you go to a restaurant, you could go to a restaurant and start talking to people perhaps although less so, whereas now takeaway you just go in, get your food, and take it back into your ready-made group and and eat and talk with the people in that group.
PETER BURCH: I think this is typical of our society, isn't it? We we tend to avoid people rather than to to seek out company; we we prefer to withdraw and sit . . .
PAM COOK: Yes, because I mean how often does one go to a restaurant in a big group like the Chinese do? I mean the Chinese when they go out they take everyone from the smallest child – aunts, uncles, the lot. It's a wonderful occasion. But I mean you know you don't see this very often. You do have sort of um the grand occasion where you're all got the carnations laid out on the table and speeches and everything but I mean you know just . . .
PETER BURCH: Very rare.
PAM COOK: Very rare. No, I mean this does happen as a social occasion, Peter.
PETER BURCH: Births, marriages and deaths.
PAM COOK: Yes, but how often does it happen as a just a whole lot of people together go go out and have a meal? Not very often.

Topic Five

DARRYL WHITELEY: Very rarely.

Edited Transcript

DARRYL WHITELEY: I think takeaway restaurants are part of the lack of sociability that's increasing all the time. Take pubs for instance. At one time you could go into a pub where you didn't know anybody and you'd expect to get into conversation with somebody there. Now they're places to go to in a group; people don't mix with the other groups there, they just go in their group. Similarly in takeaway restaurants you go in, get your food and take it away without going outside your own group.

PETER BURCH: I think this is typical of our society, isn't it? We tend to avoid people rather than seek them out.

PAM COOK: I agree. How often do people go to a restaurant in a big group like the Chinese do? When the Chinese go out they take everyone from the smallest child. It's a wonderful occasion. Here you don't see this very often except for the grand occasion when you've got speeches and everything.

PETER BURCH: And they're very rare.

PAM COOK: Yes, but they do happen.

PETER BURCH: Only for births, marriages, and deaths.

PAM COOK: But how often do people go out to have a meal together as a group?

DARRYL WHITELEY: Very rarely.

Written Work

Write briefly on one of the following topics.
1. The distinctive food of my district.
2. 'Inside every fat man is a thin man trying to get out.'
3. Should we eat natural or artificial food?
4. 'The way to a man's heart is through his stomach.'
5. The links between national food and national character.
6. Food for underdeveloped countries.
7. Food isn't what it used to be.
8. A conversation between a waiter and a customer about a fly in the soup.
9. A report for a consumer association on a restaurant meal.
10. A letter asking a friend to send you some delicacies from wherever he is living.

TOPIC SIX
SPEECH

Background *Varieties of English*
Text Foreign students often complain when they first come to England that nobody seems to speak the kind of English they have been taught at school (usually that known as R.P., i.e. Received Pronunciation). For even in England there are many ways of speaking English. Mostly this is a matter of accent, that is to say, of the pronunciation of certain sounds. Apart from speakers of R.P., accents may reveal where a person comes from and whether he lives in a town or in the country; a rough guide to regional accents is given in the map on page 74, based on the work of John Wells. However, most speakers with regional accents do not speak dialects since only their pronunciation differs from the standard, not their grammar or vocabulary.

Many other factors are also revealed in speech. Age for instance; an older person's 'wireless' may be a younger person's 'radio' or 'transistor'. Sex also: 'great' is supposed to be a man's comment, 'divine' a woman's. Perhaps the largest variation is that of social class: 'dinner' may mean a meal taken in the middle of the day or in the evening, depending on whether the speaker has working-class or middle-class eating habits. Even grammar may be affected by this: 'Can you show me that?' is interpreted by a working-class child as a question and by a middle-class child as an order.

Outside England the varieties of English are even more diverse. Australian English, American English, Indian English – the list includes practically all parts of the world where England was once influential. Each variety has its own characteristics of pronunciation, vocabulary and grammar. An American walks on the sidewalk, an Englishman on the pavement; a 'bush' is a short woody plant to an Englishman, a dense forest to a New Zealander. All of these varieties have as much right to be called English as those spoken in England, even including R.P.

Topic Six

Facts
i) When English people were asked to evaluate different accents in terms of status, they put Received Pronunciation, North American, and French at the top, and Indian, Cockney (London), and Birmingham at the bottom.
ii) 250 million people speak English as their mother tongue.
iii) 90 per cent of French scientists make use of books written in English for their research.

Points to Consider
a) Does your own language vary as much as English? In the same ways or in different ways?
b) What are the advantages of an international language? Is English an international language?
c) What variety of English do you want to learn? Why?

Dialogue 1 *Prejudice*
Listen to this conversation between husband and wife; then repeat it in small sections and discuss the points that arise.

PAUL: Good heavens!
JEAN: What?
PAUL: There's a story in the paper that a man didn't get a job because of his Australian accent.
JEAN: Well I suppose it could be a disadvantage. It depends on the job.
PAUL: This was a job as a maths teacher.
JEAN: Do you want English children to have Australian accents?
PAUL: No, but a maths teacher isn't going to have much effect, I would have thought. Specially in a secondary school.
JEAN: Yes, it does sound a bit odd. All the same, Australian is ugly.
PAUL: That's just prejudice. It shouldn't stop you getting a job.
JEAN: Nevertheless I tend to judge people by the way they speak.
PAUL: That's different. Of course one tells people's characters from the way they speak. But I hope the days are past when we used to automatically notice whether someone had been to a public school or was middle-class or something just by the way he spoke.
JEAN: Yes, I don't think people pay much attention to it any more.

Speech

Talking Points
a) In what jobs might a non-standard accent be a disadvantage? In what jobs an advantage?
b) How much do teachers influence their pupils' language, even when not directly teaching language? Is this desirable?
c) Are people really becoming less conscious of accents?

Dialogue 2 *Spelling*
First read this conversation between a sister and two brothers silently. Then choose parts and read the conversation aloud. Finally discuss any points that arise.
WENDY: How do you spell 'judgment'?
MIKE: J.U.D.G.M.E.N.T.
WENDY: Doesn't it have an 'e' in the middle?
RICHARD: Of course it does; everybody knows that.
MIKE: No it doesn't.
WENDY: Now you've confused me: I don't know what to put.
MIKE: Does it really matter?
WENDY: Of course it matters. People judge you by your spelling.
MIKE: Some of the most brilliant people can't spell.
WENDY: Well I'm not brilliant so I don't have that excuse.
RICHARD: I've never had any problems with spelling.
MIKE: Well that certainly proves you're not brilliant.
RICHARD: Oh no it doesn't.
WENDY: Oh be quiet the pair of you. I want to get on with this letter. Can you tell me how to spell 'receive'?

Talking Points
a) What English words do you find particularly difficult to spell? Why?
b) Does spelling matter very much? In what circumstances would it matter most?
c) Are there any reliable signs that someone is 'brilliant'?

Activity 1 *Questionnaire on Speech and Accents*
Tick the answers that you agree with most.
1. Which of the following describes you best in your own language?
a) a completely 'standard' speaker

71

Topic Six

    b) a speaker with some regional accent
    c) a speaker with some regional accent and dialect
    d) a speaker differing in some other way from the 'standard'
2. Do you feel having a regional accent
    a) is an advantage?
    b) is a disadvantage?
    c) doesn't matter one way or the other?
3. Imagine that you hear eight people from different countries speaking English. Put the accents in the order of attractiveness, including your own if not given.
    a) German
    b) French
    c) American
    d) Chinese
    e) Australian
    f) Spanish
    g) Indian
    h) British (R.P.)
4. Do you think that correct English
    a) should be laid down by an academic institution?
    b) should be the English spoken by the Queen of England?
    c) should be the usage of educated speakers?
    d) is a meaningless term?
5. Is it true that
    a) middle-class and working-class people speak the same?
    b) middle-class and working-class people speak differently but just as well?
    c) middle-class people speak better than working-class?
    d) working-class people speak better than middle-class?
6. The most beautiful language is
    a) Italian.
    b) Russian.
    c) Chinese.
    d) Portuguese.
    e) some other language.
7. Learning a foreign language has to be
    a) easy.
    b) fun.
    c) difficult.
8. At school the child's progress
    a) is most affected by his language capacity.
    b) is affected to some extent by his language capacity.
    c) is unaffected by his language capacity.

Speech

Activity 2 *Speech Exercises*

1. *Whispering.* A person sitting at the back of the room makes up a sentence and whispers it to the person sitting beside him; this person whispers it to the person sitting beside him; and so on till the last person is reached. Then the original and final sentences are compared.

2. *Telephones.* The class are divided into groups of three consisting of a 'caller', an 'operator', and an 'answerer'. Each trio has to act out one of the following situations.

i) a call for the fire brigade
ii) a list of vegetables to be delivered
iii) an excuse to be late home
iv) arrangements to meet a cousin you have never seen before
v) a request for information about trains to Liverpool
vi) a call home by a student who wants more money

3. An actor who wants to work at some theatres has to show that he can act by saying 'Good morning' in fifty different ways. Each student makes up a sentence and says it to the class to convey a particular emotion. The class have to decide what emotion was conveyed and then compare it with what the person intended.

Activity 3 *Problems*

The following people think that they have problems connected with speech and accents. What, if anything, do you suggest that they should do?

1. Bill Hardy, a businessman, speaks with a very 'rough', un-educated-sounding accent: he feels this is a serious handicap to his career.

2. Mary Andrews, a five-year-old girl, still has great difficulty in making herself understood by adults because of her curious pronunciation; her parents are very worried.

3. Joseph Brown wants to be an actor but he finds great difficulty in making himself heard in large halls.

4. Karl Hochheim, a German student, speaks English fluently but with a strong accent.

5. Helen Bromsgrove has just finished university where she studied French and German. Now she wants a job where she can travel and use her languages.

6. Kuldip is an Indian girl who has recently arrived in England to join her parents. Her parents do not wish her to go to the local college to learn English although she can only speak a few words.

Topic Six

Activity 4 *Visuals*

Regional Accents in Great Britain

Photo 1 *Bertrand Russell at a Political Demonstration*
Describe what is happening. What type of English would you expect Bertrand Russell to speak? Is your opinion different if you know he is (a) a philosopher and (b) a lord?

Speech

Photo 2 *Manual Labourers*
Describe what they are doing. What kind of English would you expect them to speak?

Photo 3 *A Welsh Language Protester being Taken to Prison after a Demonstration in Court*
Describe what is happening. Would you feel as strongly as this girl about the use of your native language in your country if another language were made official?

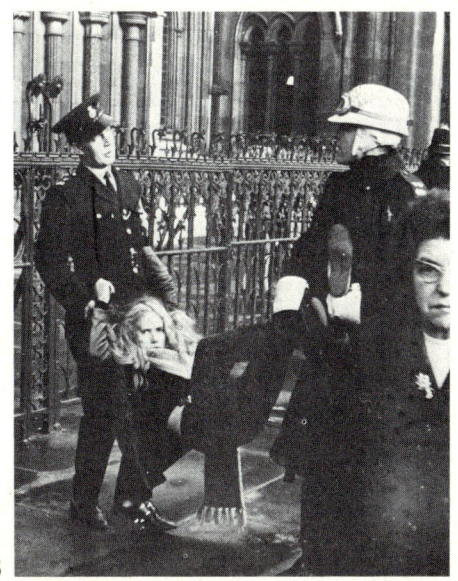

75

Topic Six

Activity 5 *Short Talks*
Prepare and give a short talk lasting two to three minutes on one of the following topics.
1. Why I am learning English.
2. The advantages of a regional accent.
3. The relationship of social class and speech.
4. The difficulties in learning English.
5. Prejudices about speech.
6. Slang.
7. Does the English language reflect the English character?
8. Which is more important, speech or writing?
9. The need for an international language.
10. Language and patriotism.

Listening Passage 1 *Class and English*
Listen to this talk about class and English. Then look at the questions. Listen to the talk again as many times as you like and answer the questions. Finally discuss any points that arise and look at the written text.

Questions
Tick the answer that fits the passage best.
1. English people a) used to worry
   b) still worry
   c) are not worried
about whether they speak correctly.
2. If you were upperclass you might own
a) a bike.
b) a cycle.
c) a horse.
3. The speaker thinks that people
a) wished to study English.
b) should pay more attention to English.
c) paid too much attention to 'U' and 'non-U'.
4. A restricted code is used for
a) expressing your own ideas.
b) writing down laws.
c) being sociable.
5. Teachers thought working-class children did badly at school because
a) they spoke restricted codes.
b) they spoke elaborated codes.
c) they didn't work well.

Speech

Discussion Points
a) How seriously should one take the distinction between 'U' and 'non-U'? How healthy is it to be interested in this?
b) Do you believe in restricted and elaborated codes? Are they found in your language?
c) How much of a handicap is working-class speech in school? If it is a handicap, should something be done about the child or about the school?

Written Text
The English have always been singularly worried about whether they are speaking correctly. Two recent examples spring to mind. One was the extraordinary national passion in the nineteen-fifties for 'U' and 'Non-U'. This started with an article by Professor Alan Ross in which he coined the terms 'U' (Upper-class) and 'Non-U' (Non-upper-class) and gave examples of differences between the two. In 'U' speech, for instance, one talked of a 'bike', not of a 'cycle'; one looked at oneself in a 'looking-glass', never in a 'mirror'. Soon all over England people were testing themselves and their friends, taking the division into 'U' and 'Non-U' much more seriously than any real student of English would wish.

The second example comes from the nineteen sixties. Another English professor, Basil Bernstein, developed a theory of language which recognised two distinct forms, called 'restricted' and 'elaborated' codes. A restricted code is used to make people feel part of a group and consists of greetings and talk about the weather and so on. An elaborated code is used to express personal opinions and original ideas. It was claimed that middle-class people used mostly the elaborated code and working-class people the restricted code. A working-class child would do badly in school because he was used to the wrong kind of code for the school environment.

Listening *Regional Accents*
Passage 2 The speakers in this live conversation are Peter Burch and Darryl Whiteley, both lecturers in German, and Mrs Pam Cook, a housewife and ex-teacher. They are discussing English regional accents and the extent to which these are now acceptable. Peter Burch starts by imitating a Northern accent and they then talk about the advantages of some regional accents compared to town accents like Cockney and about the

Topic Six

effects of 'overspill' (moving people away from town centres to the countryside).

Listen to the conversation and then look at the exercise. Listen to the conversation again as many times as you need to do the exercise. Then discuss the points that arise and look at the written transcript. There are two versions of the transcript, edited and unedited.

Exercise

Agree or disagree with these statements by saying 'Yes' or 'No'.
1. The first speaker, Peter Burch, suggests that the other speakers have regional accents.
2. He feels that most people adapt their regional accents to the standard form.
3. The second speaker, Darryl Whiteley, thinks that all regional accents are an equal disadvantage.
4. He himself dislikes Cockney.
5. He claims that managers in a new town were prejudiced against Cockney.
6. Pam Cook thinks that this shouldn't happen.
7. She thinks that some Cockney speakers are very pleasant.
8. She insists that you can separate accents from individual people.

Discussion Points

a) Would you adapt your accent in the way the speakers talk about? Why?
b) What accents do you find 'ugly'? Is there really such a thing as an 'ugly' accent?
c) To what extent are our reactions to people governed by stereotypes of 'accents' etc.?

Unedited Transcript

PETER BURCH: If you normally speak like this and you come from somewhere up North, then obviously if you come to London and, as Viv says, you you want to enter er er the Stock Exchange, you you may retain some timbre, some suggestion, of your origin because you're still proud er of of your region, but nevertheless it will be adapted very considerably to to conform with this perceived standard, wouldn't wouldn't you say so?

DARRYL WHITELEY: Well yes I think that some some backgrounds though you're you're put at rather a disadvantage. I mean it's all right, you can be proud of having of coming from Yorkshire and retaining just a faint flavour of say Yorkshire or Somerset or areas like that, but I don't think, for example, it applies to Cockney.

PETER BURCH: Yes I mean my . . .

PAM COOK: Oh why why not?

DARRYL WHITELEY: Well I I've got no objection to it but I think you'll find people do. There's partic, they did studies in a in a new town where London overspill had moved in and asked managers 'Have you got anything against somebody with a regional accent?' and he said 'No' and then qualified it by saying 'Provided it's not Cockney.'

PETER BURCH: Yes.

DARRYL WHITELEY: And I think I think there's there is still something working against London.

PAM COOK: Oh I think that's most unfair because . . .

DARRYL WHITELEY: Well obviously.

PAM COOK: I think that um obviously the Cockney accent was a shock, um if you're not used to it, but when you find that the person is such a delightful person that er you can't separate the accent from the person – they go together, and I think people should realise this.

Edited Transcript

PETER BURCH: If you have a broad accent and you come from somewhere up North and you come to London and want to work at the Stock Exchange, you will adapt your accent to conform to the perceived standard. If you're proud of your region, you may retain some suggestion of it.

DARRYL WHITELEY: Yes, but some accents are still a disadvantage. You can be proud of coming from Yorkshire or Somerset and retaining just a flavour of an accent but the same isn't true of Cockney.

PAM COOK: Why not?

DARRYL WHITELEY: Well I've got no objections to it. There was some research in a new town where people from London had moved. They asked managers whether they had anything against somebody with a regional accent and they said no. Then they qualified it by saying 'Provided it wasn't Cockney'.

PAM COOK: I think that's most unfair.

DARRYL WHITELEY: Of course it is.

79

Topic Six

PAM COOK: Obviously the Cockney accent is a shock if you're not used to it. But when you find the person speaking it is so delightful, you can't separate the accent from the person. I think people should realise this.

Written Work
Write briefly on one of the following topics.
1. What is 'good' English?
2. Learning a foreign language.
3. Problems of communication in modern society.
4. Language and nationality.
5. Prejudices about people's speech.
6. What variety of English should one learn?
7. Are we taught to speak or do we just learn to speak?
8. Two letters about exactly the same topic, one to a friend, one to your boss.
9. 'Speech is the mirror of thought.'
10. A conversation between two speakers of very different forms of English, such as a university professor and a bus-driver, or a film-star and a taxi-driver.

TOPIC SEVEN
JOBS

Background Text *Choosing a Career* (extract from 'Careers in Unilever 1973')
Choosing a career is like any other activity – it is best to work to a plan. Too many people start looking for a specific job before thinking out their occupational aims. It is a good idea to begin by attempting to define in clear terms what your requirements are from a career. This involves taking a realistic view of yourself – not only your likes and dislikes but also your strengths and weaknesses. You may think, for example, that you would like a job which involves organizing people, but liking such a job is not a sufficient justification if experience you may already have suggests that this is not your strong point. On the other hand you should remember that training will equip you to do new things. A further point to consider is how far you will be willing to do for a time things which you do not like knowing that they are necessary to achieve your longer-term objectives.

Having thought carefully about the sort of person you are, try to work out a realistic set of occupational requirements. In particular you can answer two important questions:
FIRST: what sort of life do you want to lead? For example, do you want to live in the country or in the town? Is leisure time of great importance to you? Is the size of your salary important? Do you want to put down roots or travel widely?
SECOND: what sort of work do you want to do? For example, do you like working alone or with others? Does teaching people appeal to you? Do you want to be an organizer of other people's activities? Do you want to develop new ideas and initiate change?

Facts
i) In 1971 91 per cent of men working in England worked more than 37 hours a week, 45 per cent of women.
ii) In Britain over the four year period 1968–1972 968 days per 1,000 workers were lost because of strikes; this compares with 1,912 in Italy and 56 in the Netherlands.
iii) In 1971 nine out of ten English working people said they

81

were fairly or very satisfied with their jobs; 11 per cent said they were intending to change jobs.

Points to Consider
a) How do the hours worked by men and women in your country compare with those in England?
b) What do you think of the advice on choosing a career? Have you followed a similar plan?
c) Would you say that about the same proportion of people are satisfied with their jobs in your country?

Dialogue 1 *Changing Jobs*
Listen to this conversation between husband and wife; then repeat it in small sections and discuss the points that arise.
JILL: Have you seen this job in the paper?
SIMON: The one in Manchester? Yes, I saw it.
JILL: Well aren't you going to apply? It's the kind of thing you've been looking for, isn't it?
SIMON: I hadn't really thought of it. There seem to be too many snags.
JILL: What snags?
SIMON: Well moving house for a start.
JILL: I'm the one that would affect and I can't say that I mind.
SIMON: Then there's the area. I don't fancy the idea of living in another big city.
JILL: The country around is quite pleasant, I believe.
SIMON: Well then there's the job itself.
JILL: It sounds all right. What's wrong with it?
SIMON: I can't put my finger on it but it sounds a bit odd.
JILL: You'd be more or less independent, wouldn't you?
SIMON: I suppose so. Perhaps as you're so enthusiastic I'd better find out some more about it.
JILL: You can't do any harm sending for particulars.

Talking Points
a) What reasons should one have for changing jobs? Which reasons apply to Simon?
b) Which of the snags he mentions seems to you most important? What kind of snag would prevent you from taking an otherwise attractive job?
c) Whose opinion should count in a decision about jobs? The husband's or the wife's? In other types of decision?

Jobs

Dialogue 2 *Pleasing the Boss*

First read this conversation between three colleagues silently. Then choose parts and read the conversation aloud. Finally discuss any points that arise.

BILL: I've had about all I can stand.
DEREK: What's the matter now?
BILL: Well you know Jones told me to write that report on the Bournemouth branch? I gave it to him this morning and he put it straight into the waste-paper basket.
DEREK: That's a bit much.
BILL: Well it's the last report I do for him.
PETER: Oh he's not so bad really.
BILL: You just wait till he throws one of *your* reports in the waste-paper basket.
PETER: I get on with him all right.
BILL: Well I'm glad he likes someone.
PETER: Actually I wrote a report on Bournemouth last week. Perhaps that's why he didn't need yours.
BILL: What? Do you mean to say I needn't have done it in the first place? That's the last straw. I'm going to find somewhere to work where the boss is a human being.
DEREK: Take it easy.

Talking Points

a) What do you think of Jones' behaviour? Do you think that Bill is in the right?

b) What are the best ways to handle the employer/employee relationship?

c) Is working in an office mostly paper work or are human relationships as important as elsewhere?

Activity 1 *Questionnaire*

Tick the answers that you agree with most. The questions are phrased to apply to people who already have jobs; if you do not have a job, answer in terms of the job you hope to have or the one you once had.

1. How many hours a week should people work?
a) less than 30
b) 30 to 40
c) 40 to 50
d) more than 50

2. Should the pay for a job be based on
a) the importance of the job to society?

83

Topic Seven

    b) the number of hours worked a week?
    c) the interest of the job?
    d) the number of subordinates?
    e) the amount produced?
3. Should women doing the same job as men get
    a) less pay?
    b) the same pay?
    c) more pay?
4. People should retire from work
    a) at about 60.
    b) at about 70.
    c) when they like.
    d) never.
5. People without jobs are
    a) stupid.
    b) unlucky.
    c) lazy.
    d) immoral.
6. Is your job
    a) more important to you than your spare time?
    b) less important to you than your spare time?
    c) of no importance to you?
7. Do you regard your job chiefly as
    a) a way of earning money?
    b) a means of serving others?
    c) the main method of fulfilling yourself?
8. Would you prefer a job that was mostly
    a) working with your hands?
    b) meeting people?
    c) sitting at a desk?
    d) telling other people what to do?
    e) none of these?
9. Did you choose your job because of
    a) its interest?
    b) its salary?
    c) its value to society?
    d) the prospects for promotion?
    e) the opportunities for travel?
    f) other reasons?
10. Which of the following (or the equivalent in your country) would you rather be? Put them in order of preference.
    a) Prime Minister
    b) a pop singer

c) the head of a large business firm
d) a famous writer
e) an engine-driver
f) a scientist
g) an air-hostess
h) a general
i) a university professor
j) a bishop

Activity 2 *Applying for a Job*
Fill out the application form either for a job in your own career or for an imaginary job.

Application for the post of:

Surname:

First Names:

Address:

Date of Birth:

Married, engaged, single:

Present employment:

Previous employment (please give dates and start with the most recent):

Education after the age of 11:

Qualifications:

Other information you would like to give:

Topic Seven

Activity 3 *Silford Chemicals*

Silford Chemicals is a large industrial firm making all kinds of chemical products. The firm has a vacancy for a senior executive and in response to newspaper advertisements the following people have applied: Bernard Williams, Michael Braintree, James Newport, and Mary Boston. The following details have been taken from their application forms.

Bernard Williams. He is aged thirty and is a university graduate. He has had two years experience in a fairly low job in industry. He says that he feels too restricted in his present job and would like more responsibility.

Michael Braintree. He is 35 and has been with Silford Chemicals for fifteen years. He started on the factory floor and worked his way up. He claims his experience in lower positions and his knowledge of the firm make him ideally suited to carry out executive duties.

James Newport. He is 54 and has had plenty of business experience in a variety of firms. He is at present working in a similar job for about the same amount of money. He wants to change for 'personal reasons'.

Mary Boston. She is 40 and started work as a secretary but transferred to an executive job. She is unmarried and writes 'I have never found any problems in telling men what to do.'

One group of students are the committee that has to interview the candidates for the job. Other students play the people mentioned above and any surprise last minute candidates whose application forms we do not have. The committee decides what questions to ask the candidates, interviews them, and decides who gets the job.

Activity 4 *Photographs*

Photo 1 *Assembling Rolls-Royce Engines*
Describe the factory and what these workers are doing. Would you like this kind of job? How can factory jobs be made more interesting?

Photo 2 *An Air-hostess on British Airways*
Describe what the passengers and the air-hostess are doing. What are the attractions of being an air-hostess?

Jobs

1

2

Topic Seven

Photo 3 *A Street Accident*
Describe the scene. What qualities would you need to be a fireman or ambulance driver?

Photo 4 *Edward Heath when he first became Prime Minister*
Describe Mr Heath's appearance and expression. Do you think politics is an interesting career?

3

4

Jobs

Activity 5 *Short talks*
Prepare and give a short talk lasting two to three minutes on one of the following topics.
1. My present job.
2. What I would most like to be.
3. How a knowledge of English is useful to my job.
4. The job I would most hate to do.
5. Why I would make a suitable Prime Minister/President.
6. 'Woman's place is in the home.'
7. How important is one's job?
8. Which is nobler – working with the hands or the mind?
9. It isn't what one *does* but what one *is* that matters.
10. How to get the job you want.

Listening *A Varied Career*
Passage 1 Listen to this talk about a novelist. Then look at the questions. Listen to the story again as many times as you need to answer the questions. Finally discuss any points that arise and look at the written text.

Questions
Tick the answer that fits the passage best.
1. Paperbacks
a) are a kind of money.
b) often have short biographies.
c) are biographies you pick up.
2. Macintyre doesn't want to embarrass
a) his parents.
b) his readers.
c) his school.
3. The places where authors live are always
a) unnamed.
b) famous.
c) amazing.
4. The photo
a) includes the author.
b) is wonderful.
c) is surprising.
5. On the cover there is
a) the story of the book.
b) the price of the book.
c) the story of the author.

Topic Seven

Discussion Points
a) Have you read biographies like this? What is the point of them?
b) Do writers write from their own experience or from their imagination? How can you tell which is which?
c) What are the advantages of trying a number of jobs before settling down in one?

Written Text
Whenever you pick up a paperback, you seem to find a short biography of the author. You know the sort of thing. 'James Macintyre, the son of an English ambassador and a South American gypsy, attended one of England's most famous schools which he will not name because of the embarrassment it might cause them. His first job was as a waiter in a well-known Paris hotel; then, after nearly losing his life in a fight with the captain of the cattle-boat he was working on, he became a private detective and bus-driver and began to write adventure stories in his spare time, based on his experiences. He now lives quietly in the country with his wife, three daughters, and a cat called Fritz; he spends much of his time practising the violin.'

They really are extraordinary, these authors! The amazing things that happen to them in such deliberately vague foreign parts. Ten years ago there must have been more novelists on cattle-boats than cattle. And what is even more marvellous is the photo of the author sometimes included. Can this dreamy looking person really have fought the tough captain of a cattle-boat and survived? At any rate, whatever the actual novel's like, you've had your money's worth in the story printed on the cover.

Listening *Job Satisfaction*
Passage 2 This is an extract from a live conversation between Miss Jenny Drew and Mrs Jennifer Bagg. They are both at present students studying for an external university degree at a polytechnic; Mrs Bagg was formerly a nurse. They are talking about job satisfaction – how people can find their work rewarding.

Listen to the conversation and then look at the exercise. Listen to the conversation again as many times as you need to

Jobs

do the exercise. Then discuss the points that arise and look at the written transcript. There are two versions, edited and unedited.

Exercise
Agree or disagree with these statements by saying 'Yes' or 'No'.
1. The first speaker, Mrs Bagg, thinks it is bad to be bored by one's job.
2. She believes that leisure time is more important than your job.
3. The second speaker, Jenny Drew, implies that Mrs Bagg wants to be a journalist.
4. She feels that monotonous jobs can nevertheless be rewarding.
5. Mrs Bagg thinks that their disadvantage is that they don't change and develop.
6. Jenny Drew believes that a job should involve working with people.

Discussion Points
a) What do you think makes a satisfying job? How can jobs be made more satisfying?
b) Why do people choose particular careers?
c) What jobs are working 'with' people and what are working 'among' people? Which do you prefer?

Unedited Transcript
MRS BAGG: I think job, you know your job is important and if you're going to be bored, you know, if you're going to do it for the rest of your life, it's very sad. So I don't think you want it to be everything to you but you want it to be pretty important – as important as your leisure time – because you spend far more of your time doing it. But what makes it a good job or a satisfying job I don't know; it's obviously entirely different for everybody.

JENNY DREW: It's all right if you've got a career that you want to follow, I suppose, if you're very interested in journalism or something and you want to, or be a nurse, at least it's something that you've often wanted to be, but there's so many jobs concerned with just working in factories, filling in forms, working in offices that . . .

MRS BAGG: There's no incentive involved; you're not getting anywhere.

Topic Seven

JENNY DREW: There's no job satisfaction at all.

MRS BAGG: You're static; in fact you're sort of earning more money to start off with than you will later on and you're doing the same job.

JENNY DREW: You're not even working with people a lot of – well you're working amongst people; it's entirely different from working with people.

Edited Transcript

MRS BAGG: I think your job is important. If you're going to do a job that bores you for the rest of your life, it's very sad. You don't want your job to be everything to you but you want it to be pretty important – as important as your leisure time – because you spend far more of your time working. I don't know what makes a good job or a satisfying job; it's obviously entirely different for everybody.

JENNY DREW: It's all right if you want to follow a particular career. If you've always wanted to be a nurse or a journalist and that is what you're doing, that's fine. But there are so many jobs that are just working in factories or offices, filling in forms and so on.

MRS BAGG: Yes there's no incentive; you're not getting anywhere; you're static in fact. You're doing the same job all the time. In fact you earn more money when you first start work than you will later.

JENNY DREW: You're not even working with people a lot of the time; you may be working *among* people but that's entirely different from working *with* people.

Written Work

Write briefly on one of the following topics.
1. A typical day in my job.
2. A successful man.
3. 'All work and no play make Jack a dull boy.'
4. Does a person have a right to choose his own job?
5. 'Equal pay for equal work.'
6. The needs of the individual and the needs of society.
7. The problem of unemployment.
8. Strikes.
9. An advertisement for a job you would like.
10. A letter of application for a job.

TOPIC EIGHT
SPORTS & GAMES

Background Text *Australia v. Indonesia in the Federation Cup* (extract reproduced from *The Times*, 5.v.1973 by permission)
Australia lost only one set to Indonesia. Evonne Goolagong won the first set 6-0 against Lany Kaligis, but then made four errors to lose her service to love in the first game of the second set. Miss Kaligis, who has a big hat, a big smile, and a big heart, has been around long enough to know that Miss Goolagong's concentration was wandering. The Indonesian promptly made the most of her chance and won that set 7-5. That fleeting set-back inspired Miss Goolagong to regain her best form. With her wonderful flowing ease, she quietly and gracefully pushed the match to its inevitable if deferred conclusion. Pat Coleman, only 19 years old, and on her second international tour, admirably passed a test of nerve and concentration in the second singles, against the ambidextrous Lita Sugiarto, formerly Miss Liem. The Indonesian played badly. But Miss Coleman's reaction to the occasion was nevertheless impressive.

Facts
i) Football matches in the Football League in England attract about thirty million spectators a year; about one million amateurs play football. However, there are about three million people who go fishing in England.
ii) In a Government Survey carried out in the 1960s English people said that they spent 23 per cent of their leisure time watching television; the men said they spent 11 per cent playing sport and 3 per cent watching sport, the women 4 per cent playing and 1 per cent watching.
iii) The responsibility for sport in Great Britain rests with three Sports Councils, for England, Scotland and Wales, who are primarily concerned with distributing the four million pounds a year made available by the national government.

Topic Eight

Points to Consider
a) How great a proportion of leisure is spent on sport in your country?
b) Which are the most popular sports in your country both for spectators and for participants?
c) How useful are international competitions like the Federation Cup?

Dialogue 1 *Footballers' Pay*
Listen to this conversation between three friends; then repeat it in small sections and discuss the points that arise.

JULIAN: I really don't see why footballers get such high salaries.

BOB: Neither do I. After all how much work do they do? A couple of hours a week.

DAVID: Well it's a kind of entertainment, I suppose. The money that film stars and pop singers get is just as ridiculous.

JULIAN: And it affects the sport. The players are thinking all the time how much money they're taking home and how much they're worth if they transfer to another club.

DAVID: Yes, it's not the team that counts any more.

BOB: But it's funny how the fans still follow a club.

JULIAN: I wasn't thinking of that so much as the actual way the game's played. Nowadays it's a series of individuals doing clever things with the ball but no teamwork.

BOB: Oh I'm not so certain of that. To win you've still got to play as a team. I remember only last month when West Ham played Wolves . . .

Talking Points
a) How much money should sportsmen get for sport? Do you agree that footballers get too much?
b) How much does the team count and how much the individual player? Should players be loyal to a club or team?
c) Has the style of sport changed in recent years? In what ways?

Dialogue 2 *Women's Sport*
First read this conversation between three friends silently. Then choose parts and read it aloud. Finally discuss any points that arise.

DIANA: Did you see the gymnastics on television last night? The Russian girls were very good, I thought.

Sports & Games

BARRY: Yes, it's nice to see a sport in which women are actually superior to men.
DIANA: That's the kind of thing only a man would say. Some women are very good at sport.
BARRY: Only at the sports that don't need strength. Have you ever seen women playing football? It's pathetic.
STEVEN: Not all sports need strength. Women are good at things that need grace and skill. Like gymnastics.
DIANA: That's right: different but equal.
BARRY: I'm not so certain. Even in the sports that need grace, a good man is often better than a good woman.
DIANA: But look at skating. Men make skating a display of muscles.
STEVEN: Yes, skating's like dancing. And there women definitely excel.
BARRY: There have been male ballet dancers, you know.
DIANA: Really, men are impossible! Nothing but prejudice.

Talking Points
a) Which sports need strength, which grace?
b) Should women play all sports or only some? Why?
c) What is the difference between sport and art? Is skating a sport? Ballet? Gymnastics?

Activity 1 *Questionnaire*
Tick the answers you agree with most.
1. International sport is important because
a) people from different countries can meet each other.
b) countries can show how good they are.
c) it's cheaper and less harmful than wars.
d) it sets a standard for playing sports.
e) it makes money for the organizing country.
2. Sport is important to the individual because
a) it keeps him healthy.
b) it builds his character.
c) it gives him something to do with his leisure.
d) it enables him to meet people.
3. People who play sports should be
a) unpaid amateurs.
b) paid a certain amount but not enough to live on.
c) paid by the government.
d) professionals who earn their living by sport.

Topic Eight

4. The most important aspect of an indoor game is
a) its educational value.
b) its amusement value.
c) the time it takes.
d) its cheapness.
5. Which type of sports do you prefer?
a) sports in which one individual usually competes against another individual (e.g. tennis)
b) sports in which teams compete against each other (e.g. football)
c) sports in which there is usually no direct competition between individuals or teams (e.g. recreational skiing)
6. Which are the most popular games in your country?
a) card games such as bridge or canasta
b) board games such as chess and draughts
c) commercially produced games such as Scrabble and Monopoly
d) none of these
7. Do you prefer to
a) watch other people playing sport?
b) play sport yourself?
c) watch sport on television?
d) have nothing to do with sport?
8. Do you think people who are not interested in sport are
a) lazy?
b) silly?
c) sensible?

Activity 2 *Classroom Games*

A. *Consequences*

The most common way of playing this is to make up a story about two people who meet in a particular place and talk to each other, and the consequences that follow. A long piece of paper is handed out to each player.

i) First write the name of a man (the hero of the story) at the top of the paper, followed by the word 'met'. The name can be real or fictional, alive or dead, famous or unknown, e.g.

    William Shakespeare met

Then fold the piece of paper over towards you so that the words cannot be read and pass it on to the person sitting beside you.

Sports & Games

ii) Now write the name of a woman (the heroine), fold and pass, e.g.
    Elizabeth Taylor

iii) Write a short phrase giving the place where the characters met, fold and pass, e.g.
    in the Tower of London

iv) Write 'He said to her . . .' and supply what he said, fold and pass, e.g.
    He said to her 'Do you know the way to the zoo?'

v) Write 'She said to him . . .' and supply what she said, fold and pass, e.g.
    She said to him 'How dare you!'

vi) Write 'And the consequences were . . .' and supply what you think happened afterwards, fold and pass, e.g.
    And the consequences were the Prime Minister resigned.

vii) Now unfold the piece of paper you have and read the story aloud.

The game can be played in many different ways, by varying the details of the story, by using drawings instead of words, and so on.

B. *I Spy*

One person decides on an object that can be seen in the classroom and declares 'I spy with my little eye something beginning with . . .' and gives the first letter of the word. The other players have to discover what it is by asking questions 'Is it a . . .', e.g.

I spy with my little eye something beginning with B.
Is it a blackboard? No.
Is it a book? Yes, it is.

This game may be made more difficult by using objects visible in some place known to all the players rather than those in the classroom itself.

C. *Twenty Questions*

One person thinks of an object and announces whether it is 'Animal, Vegetable, Mineral, or Abstract'; the other players have to discover what it is by asking questions. The questions must all have the answer 'Yes' or 'No'. If the object has not been discovered in twenty questions the person has won. The only tricky point about this game is to remember that *all* things have to be either animal, vegetable, mineral or abstract,

Topic Eight

that is to say a table is vegetable, a person is animal. An alternative way of playing it is 'Twenty Statements'; each player thinks of something and describes it in twenty short statements. The other players have to guess what it is before he says all twenty.

D. *Ghosts*

The first person thinks of a word, e.g. 'cricket', but gives only the first letter which is written on the blackboard by the teacher, e.g.

   C

The next person has to try to guess the word and give the next letter, e.g.

   C H

The object of the game is not to finish a word; a person who finishes a word becomes a 'ghost'; the winner is the last person who is not a ghost. A 'word' is longer than two letters; it does not matter what the person intended if the result is an English word, e.g. a player wanted to make FAI into FAIRY so he added R but this meant he had finished the word FAIR and became a ghost. One important rule is that, if a player cannot think how to continue, he can 'challenge' the previous player to name the word he was thinking of; if this player names a word, the player who challenged becomes a ghost; if he cannot give one, then *he* becomes a ghost. Two variations are: (a) human beings cannot speak to ghosts and become ghosts if a ghost can make them speak, (b) 'Superghosts', in which words can be built up at the beginning or in the middle as well as at the end.

Activity 3   *The Best Sportsman*

Each student draws up a list of the best sportsman ever in as many as possible of the following sports. Then the most popular names in each sport are put up on the blackboard and the students decide, by voting if necessary, who is the best of all.

a) Football
b) Skiing
c) Cycling
d) Athletics
e) Swimming
f) Skating
g) Gymnastics
h) Tennis

Sports & Games

Activity 4   *Photographs*

Photo 1   *Jean Claud Killy at the Grenoble Winter Olympics*
Describe his appearance and equipment. Do you think skiing is dangerous?

Photo 2   *Police separating fighting footballers*
Describe what the police and the players are doing. Should this kind of thing happen in sport?

1

2

Topic Eight

Photo 3 *A motor-racing crash*
Describe what is happening. Why do drivers want to compete in motor-racing?

Photo 4 *Miss Evonne Goolagong*
Describe Miss Goolagong. To what extent is tennis a spectator sport?

Sports & Games

Activity 5 *Short talks*
Prepare and give a short talk lasting two to three minutes on one of the following topics.
1. The worst umpire or referee I have ever seen.
2. My favourite sportsman/sportswoman.
3. The sport I like best.
4. Is hunting a sport?
5. Gambling.
6. It's playing the game, not winning it, that's important.
7. West Ham United is the best football team in the world.
8. Sportsmen use their muscles, not their brains.
9. Horse-racing is the sport of kings.
10. Life is just a game.

Listening Passage 1 *A Football Commentary*
Listen to this commentary on a football match between Newbury and Silford. Then look at the questions. Listen to the commentary again as many times as you need to answer the questions. Finally discuss any points that arise and look at the written text.

Questions
Tick the answer that fits the passage best.
1. Baynes is a) the referee.
   b) a Silford player.
   c) a Newbury player.
2. Franks a) scores a goal.
   b) runs away.
   c) has a rifle.
3. The match is a) won by Silford.
   b) won by Newbury.
   c) a draw.
4. Franks a) kicked the ball.
   b) took it home.
   c) hit it with a hammer.
5. King's mistake was a) to handle the ball.
   b) to hit the upright.
   c) to let Franks have the ball.

Discussion Points
a) Can you really follow a football match from a sports commentary? What would make an ideal commentary?
b) Do you think this was a good match? Why?
c) To what extent is football an individual game?

Topic Eight

Written Text

The ball goes far into the Newbury defence. It's picked up in midfield by Peter Watt. He loses it. No, he chases it. He's going down the line. He turns it and it's headed up in the air by one of the Newbury defenders. Finally it's brought down by Baynes, the captain of the Newbury side, who sends it downfield to Franks, far inside the Silford half. King has got it for Silford; he turns; no, Franks has taken it away; King has got himself in terrible trouble. Franks is going away. He shoots and it's there. Franks makes it Newbury 3 Silford nil. Franks accelerated twenty yards and then hammered it home with his right foot. Not many goalkeepers could have stopped that sort of shot. It spun off his hands, hit the upright and bounced into the back of the net. I must say Newbury tonight are a very different team from the one we saw at Brighton last week. And what a mistake by one of the best defenders in England. He simply gave Franks the ball and he seized his chance; there was no danger at all.

Listening Passage 2 *My Favourite Sportswoman*

The speaker in this live talk is Richard Parry, a student studying for an external university degree at a polytechnic. He was asked to speak on one of the topics given on page 101; he chose 'My favourite sportswoman' and spoke about Miss Evonne Goolagong, the Australian tennis player, whose photograph appears on page 100. He describes her background and early career and her visits to the Wimbledon tennis championship in England. On her second visit there she beat Margaret Court on the Centre Court to become the women's champion.

Listen to the talk and then look at the exercise. Listen to the talk again as many times as you need to do the exercise. Then discuss the points that arise and look at the written transcript.

Exercise

Agree or disagree with these statements by saying 'Yes' or 'No'.
1. Miss Goolagong came from the city of Sidney.
2. She started to compete in tournaments when she was very young.
3. On her first visit she became Wimbledon champion.
4. On her second visit she was beaten very early on.
5. In the final with Margaret Court she played very well to begin with.
6. It was a very long match.

Sports & Games

7. She always appears cheerful and good-mannered while playing.
8. Even if she never wins again, people will remember her.

Discussion Points
a) What kinds of background do successful sportsmen and women often come from?
b) What is the ideal temperament to win sports events like Wimbledon? Do you think Miss Goolagong possesses it?
c) How much does it help a player if he knows that the crowd is supporting him rather than his opponent?

Unedited Transcript
My favourite sportswoman is Australian tennis star Evonne Goolagong. She was born twenty-one years ago in a small village in the wheat country outside Sidney in New South Wales, Australia. She was born of a white father and part-aborigine mother and they encouraged her during her early years to take up tennis and in fact by the age of six she already had most of the shots although her tennis implements were rather crude. By the time she was ten, she was entering in the junior tournaments in and around the Sidney area and it was at one of these that she first attracted the attention of Victor Edwards, a well-known Australian coach; he immediately recognised her natural talent and potential, and sought to take her under his wing. Well, under Mr Edwards' guidance she blossomed into a very fine player indeed, although at times her natural ability and her habits that she had formed tended to get the better of what she'd been coached to do, but she managed to win several tournaments in Australia and in New Zealand as well and at the age of eighteen she came to Wimbledon for the first time. Well, although she got knocked out in the second round of the competition proper, she managed to win the Plate event, and, having tasted success at Wimbledon, she also won a couple of other tournaments in Great Britain. Well, she was back a year later and this time came through the first week of Wimbledon without any problems at all and people began to sit up and take notice. On the Monday of the second week in the quarter-finals she beat Nancy Richey; on the Wednesday she beat Billie-Jean King; and on the Friday she was to meet Margaret Court, a fellow-Australian and arguably the best woman tennis-player in the world. The whole of the Centre Court desperately wanted Evonne to win and probably

thought that her best chance was the fact that Margaret Court is a very bad starter. But Evonne started superbly and was four games to love up before Margaret knew what was going on and in many ways it was a sort of rush of success for Evonne that kept Margaret right out of the game and forty minutes later it was all over and Wimbledon had a new champion and the Centre Court had a new darling.

All Evonne's opponents who play her on the Centre Court remark about how firmly the crowd tends to be in the Australian's favour and the reasons for this aren't hard to see – she smiles a lot on court, acknowledges her opponents' good shots, and has this sort of happy-go-lucky air that's lent itself to many stories about her, such as her humming to herself on court, and being forgetful, and er tending to stand at the wrong places at the wrong time for receiving serve. After her Wimbledon triumph er two years ago her coach said it was possibly the last time she'd ever win Wimbledon: she's that sort of person. Someone once called her 'instant spring'. Well even if she doesn't win Wimbledon again and doesn't go on to be one of the world's greatest ever players, I think she'll still be fondly remembered by everyone who ever saw her.

Written Work
Write briefly on one of the following topics.
1. The importance of sport.
2. The game I enjoy most.
3. Sport and politics.
4. People's true character is revealed in games.
5. The provision of sports facilities.
6. Should sports like boxing be banned?
7. Which is more important – to watch or to take part?
8. A newspaper description of a football match or other sporting event.
9. A conversation between two sports fans about their favourite sport.
10. A letter of admiration to your favourite sportsman or sportswoman.

TOPIC NINE
FASHION & POP

Background Text

Summer Fashion

The extract that follows is taken from *Brides and Setting Up Home*, early summer, 1973. It is about an English fashion designer, Lee Bender, who designs clothes for a chain of boutiques called Bus Stop and is a supporter of the Woman's Liberation Movement.

'It's going to be a cream summer' predicts Lee Bender ... Lee is an independent designer and although her clothes sometimes reflect St Laurent's style, she maintains that this is purely coincidental ... She admires natural colours, such as black, white, grey and brown and strong geometric prints, Hawaiian flowers and flamingoes are characteristic of her designs in a season when little tight flower prints are around in abundance ... Big hats are not her favourites – perhaps because they conjure up a picture of unliberated dress. She considers small hats are much more in keeping with the new mood ... Colours to wear with cream? 'Keep a total look' she advises. 'I think that everything should be cream, including jewellery' ... Lee Bender likes to see make-up, painted eyes and a delicious brown skin ... I asked the designer how she thought women would react to the return of more classic clothes. She said candidly that, commercially speaking, she hoped that it would catch on, but freedom in dress, like any other form of liberation, is very difficult to give up.

Points to Consider
a) What designers like Lee Bender are there in your country? Are they independent or do they largely follow Paris or London fashions?
b) To what extent is the colour of the clothes you are going to wear the first thing that comes to your mind?
c) What would you say was 'liberated' dress? Can you be 'liberated' in dress if you follow the advice of professional fashion designers?

Dialogue 1 *Pop Music*
Listen to this conversation between two pop fans; then repeat it in small sections and discuss the points that arise.
BOB: I still think the Beatles are the greatest ever.
FRANK: Well they were all right in their time, I suppose. But somehow they always seemed a bit sentimental. Not like the Stones.
BOB: No, you certainly couldn't accuse the Rolling Stones of being sentimental.
FRANK: That's how pop should be – tough and plenty of beat.
BOB: And melodic too.
FRANK: I don't know. 'Melodic' sounds like commercial pop for the under-tens. You know, Donny Osmond or somebody.
BOB: Oh the Osmonds are just in it for the money.
FRANK: So were all the other pop stars, apparently.
BOB: Yes, it was upsetting the way they all made millions and retired to the South of France.
FRANK: Particularly when pop was supposed to be a way of life.
BOB: I know – the alternative society, drugs, revolution, and so on.
FRANK: Well that's all over now, thank goodness, and a pop star's a pop star, not a philosopher putting the world right.

Talking Points
a) Which do you consider are the greatest pop group ever?
b) What factors make great pop music?
c) Should pop music be more than music and present political and moral ideas? Or should it just be music?

Dialogue 2 *Next Year's Fashion*
First read this conversation between three girls silently. Then choose parts and read it aloud. Finally discuss any points that arise.
HAZEL: It says in this magazine that we'll all be back to flat heels next year.
MARY: Oh no! I'd just got used to walking on these.
ANNE: I can't say *I* shall mind. I've never been so uncomfortable in my life. And the times I've fallen over!

Fashion & Pop

MARY: That means altering all my dresses.
HAZEL: And that new coat of mine, it'll be completely wrong. And I paid enough for it.
ANNE: Still they're probably wrong. It sounds like one of those fashions magazines talk about and nobody wears.
HAZEL: I hope so.
MARY: But I'll still have to get some low heels just in case.
ANNE: Well I'm not getting any. I'm going to be independent for a change.
HAZEL: You wait and see; you'll be wearing them just like the rest of us.

Talking Points
a) What do you consider is the fashionable height for shoes now?
b) What influence do fashion writers have on fashion? Do you think this is a good influence?
c) How much can you go against the fashion of the day?

Activity 1 *Questionnaire*
Tick the answers that you agree with most.
1. If you have a bright red shirt the best colour to go with it is
a) navy.
b) pink.
c) orange.
d) green.
e) yellow.
2. Eye-shadow should consist of
a) a single colour applied to the upper lid.
b) a single colour applied to the upper lid and below the eye.
c) one colour applied to the upper eyelid, another above the eyelid but below the eyebrow.
d) none of these.
3. The first thing a man notices about a woman is
a) her figure.
b) her face.
c) her clothes.
d) her perfume.
e) her voice.
f) none of these.

Topic Nine

4. The reason why women pay attention to clothes is
a) they want to look attractive to themselves.
b) they want to look attractive to men.
c) they want to make other women jealous.
d) they have been oppressed by a male-dominated society.
5) People should dress
a) to please themselves.
b) to keep up with fashion.
c) to suit their jobs.
d) to suit their social class.
e) none of these.
6. Pop music sounds best
a) on a record-player at home.
b) in a concert.
c) in a club or discotheque.
d) on the radio or television.
7) The best type of pop music is
a) 'commercial'.
b) blues.
c) progressive.
d) heavy rock.
e) none of these.
8. The greatest pop singer ever was
a) Bob Dylan.
b) Mick Jagger.
c) Elvis Presley.
d) Paul McCartney.
e) Frank Sinatra.
f) Diana Ross.
g) Joan Baez. .
h) Charles Aznavour.
i) someone else.

Activity 2   *Well-dressed People*
Describe the clothes you associate with the following people.
1. Charlie Chaplin
2. Mrs Gandhi
3. Chairman Mao Tse Tung
4. John Lennon
5. Tarzan

Fashion & Pop

    6. Astronaut Shepherd
    7. Elizabeth Taylor
    8. Queen Elizabeth II
    9. Greta Garbo
   10. Queen Elizabeth I

Activity 3 *Silford Radio*

A. Silford Radio is a small commercial radio station broadcasting to the inhabitants of Silford. Its programmes largely consist of pop music and local news. Most of the work is done by one man, Peter Henry, the programme director. During one day he has to cope with the following problems. Give him what help you can.

i) He has to compile a 'Top Ten' of listeners' favourite records. Make a list of your ten favourites and then prepare a top ten by combining all the lists together.

ii) He desperately needs local news items. Prepare some for him, remembering that they must of general interest and not controversial or libellous.

iii) From 9.00 till 11.00 Radio Silford provides a music programme of easy listening catering for all ages and tastes. Prepare a balanced list of records that he can use and put them in the best order.

B. During the day Peter Henry becomes involved in the following situations. Act out what happens.

i) A pop group called 'My Aunt Betty' arrive for a recording. They have forgotten some of their instruments and don't think they are being paid enough money.

ii) Mrs Cromwell, the leader of a local campaign to clean up radio and television, arrives in his office with a group of ladies, to protest about the 'disgusting' pop music his station broadcasts.

iii) The pop group for the programme next day cannot come. He has to phone round to discover another group that is free.

iv) Miss Dolores Rio, formerly Betty Smith, and her agent, Larry Stevens, come to him to convince him that she is the world's greatest singer. In fact she is terrible but Peter Henry does not wish to offend them.

v) Two famous pop singers, George Harrison and Paul Simon, happen to be passing through Silford. Peter Henry has to get short interviews with both of them.

Topic Nine

Activity 4 *Photographs*
Photo 1 *Dancing in a pop club*
Describe what the girl is wearing. Are pop clubs good for young people? What do you think of modern dance styles?

Photo 2 *Mick Jagger*
Describe Mick Jagger. Do you find his face attractive? What do you think he is doing?

Photo 3 *Interior of Biba boutique*
Describe the interior of this shop. Do you think boutiques like this are the best place to buy clothes? Why do you think they have become popular?

Photo 4 *Avantgarde makeup*
Describe the girl's face. Do you think this type of make-up will become common? Why do people wear make-up?

Fashion & Pop

3

4

Topic Nine

Activity 5 *Short Talks*

Prepare and give a short talk lasting two to three minutes on one of the following topics.
1. The clothes I am wearing at the moment.
2. This year's fashions.
3. The important thing about shoes is to be comfortable.
4. How to dress well without spending much money.
5. Making your own clothes.
6. The kind of pop music I like best.
7. Pop clubs.
8. Fashions in pop music.
9. Should some kinds of pop music be banned?
10. My favourite pop musician.

Listening Passage 1 *A Pop Concert*

Listen to this account of a pop concert given on Silford Radio. Then look at the questions. Listen to the passage again as many times as you like till you can answer all the questions. Then discuss any points that arise and look at the written text.

Questions

Tick the answers that fit the passage best.
1. The reporter implies that
a) the musicians had got lost.
b) the music wasn't very good.
c) the arena wasn't very full.
2. 'Sideboards' couldn't play because their lead guitarist was
a) lost.
b) trapped in a car.
c) ill.
3. The reporter says that
a) one group couldn't be heard.
b) he has a deaf aunt.
c) one group were too loud.
4. Freddie Nash is
a) a blues singer.
b) a guitarist.
c) an actor.
5. 'Ealing Broadway' are going to
a) be forgotten.
b) expand their numbers.
c) become famous.

Fashion & Pop

Discussion Points
a) What do you think of pop festivals? Do they still take place in your country?
b) How does a pop group become famous? What is the most important factor in their success?
c) Do you like music in the open air? Does all music come across in those conditions?

Written Text
We'd all heard about this fabulous one-day pop festival at Silford Hall and so there we were, all five thousand of us, and there was this open-air arena with trees and grass and things; but where was the music? First we were promised 'Sideboards', a rock band that play nineteen-fifties standards. But then we were told that 'Sideboards' had had a car crash and their lead guitarist couldn't play till he had recovered. So instead we were to have 'My Aunt Betty'. Well 'My Aunt Betty' set up their speakers and amplifiers for an hour or so and then started to play. So at last we had some music; at least those in the front row did; the rest of us couldn't hear in spite of all the fuss over the equipment. After lunch things improved slightly with the appearance of Freddie Nash – at least he sings blues as if he meant them and has an exciting stage act. But he stuck to his old successes and didn't give us anything we hadn't heard before. The rest of the day we had one dreary local group after another. The only one with any promise were 'Ealing Broadway' – a solid beat and good solos – one of those bands that'll be very big in a year or two. But, all in all, one of those days I'd rather forget.

Listening Passage 2 *Mick Jagger*
The speaker in this live talk, Mrs Jennifer Bagg, is describing the photo of Mick Jagger that appears on page 110. Mrs Bagg is at present a student in a polytechnic. After describing Mick Jagger's appearance she talks about his early career when he scandalised many people, his tours with the Rolling Stones, the 'free' concerts they gave in England and America, at one of which someone was murdered by a group called Hells Angels, the film Mick Jagger made, and his life today.

Listen to the talk and then look at the exercise. Listen again to the talk as many times as you need to do the exercise. Then discuss the points that arise and look at the written transcript.

Topic Nine

Exercise
Agree or disagree with these statements by saying 'Yes' or 'No'.
1. Mrs Bagg implies that many pop stars of the sixties are no longer famous.
2. She says that Mick Jagger is wearing sunglasses.
3. She thinks he was chiefly popular with older people.
4. Everybody liked his music.
5. The Rolling Stones have travelled very widely.
6. There was violence at their Hyde Park concert.
7. Mick Jagger was in a film called Performance.
8. She thinks that Mick Jagger is quite old now.

Discussion Points
a) Did pop music shock parents in your country? Is this still true?
b) Should 'free' concerts in the open air be allowed?
c) How many people can be as versatile as Mick Jagger who can both sing and act?

Unedited Transcript
This is a picture of Mick Jagger, a famous English pop singer, who still is famous. In this picture he looks as if he's arriving or departing from an airport. He's got an extraordinary hat on, looks like an old straw boater from school with lots of flowers tucked in it, no doubt to attract attention, and he's carrying sunglasses and a rather gaily-coloured jacket. Um he was most popular in the sixties I think, singing with a group, er five of them, and um they sort of took England by storm – all sorts of teenage girls sort of screaming and shouting and thinking they were the greatest thing, and Mick Jagger was very sexy and parents didn't really approve of him 'cos he started having long hair and very tight trousers, and the music wasn't always approved of either because it was a different sort of music really; it was, er there was a lot of beat to it; it was good for dancing, and um it said things that young people thought about and believed in and they felt that they could identify with this person. Anyway after fame in England he and his group have travelled all over the world er to the United States and to Australia and New Zealand, done big world tours, made lots of records that have sold very well, and they also give concerts. One concert in particular um was free, given in Hyde Park in London in the summer and this was attended by thousands of people. Um it was rather a beautiful day and the music was nice and it

was a rather nice thing to do. But since that time they've been banned, these sort of concerts in Hyde Park and England because I suppose there's trouble and a lot of people getting together get carried away and sometimes violence happens. This did happen in the United States at a concert that the Rolling Stones with Mick Jagger singing, concert they gave over there; um someone was actually killed while they were watching I think by some Hells Angels, which is rather a sad thing to happen. Um in addition to records um that the Rolling Stones have made Mick Jagger's been in films, er notably Performance, which was a very interesting film um where he played – there were two characters in it, both really playing the same person; it was rather interesting and novel idea and made a rather good film. I think everyone was surprised that Mick Jagger could actually act as well as sing and gyrate about the stage. Anyway he's probably getting on in years now and er he still sings and travels around, I think. Um he's married to a model called Bianca. Um I think that the Rolling Stones um have lived in France um and don't spend very much time in England but I'm not really sure.

Written Work
Write briefly on one of the following topics.
1. The price of clothes.
2. Male fashion.
3. National costume.
4. Dressing to fit the occasion.
5. The fashion industry.
6. Are pop, jazz, and blues the same?
7. Pop music and politics.
8. A record sleeve for your favourite record.
9. A letter describing a record you have just heard.
10. A description of a pop concert.

TOPIC TEN
THE ARTS

Background *Reading in England*
Text Most books in England today are bought in the form of 'paperback' rather than 'hardback' editions. The fiction that is bought probably mostly falls into the category of 'light' reading – crime and adventure stories, science fiction and romances. The most popular type of crime story used to be the 'whodunit' in which a carefully constructed plot prevented the reader from learning till the last page the identity of the murderer; two classical writers of whodunits were Agatha Christie with her Poirot stories, and Erle Stanley Gardener with his Perry Mason stories. Crime stories now tend to be fast-moving adventures in which the hero, more often a spy than a detective, fights his way through a series of impossible situations. Some writers, however, make a virtue of squalid realism, whether the spy stories of Len Deighton, or the American police routine of Ed McBain.

Science fiction also has been changing. After its early obsession with 'bug-eyed monsters' and 'space operas' about empires of the distant future, it went through a phase when it was concerned more with 'inner' space than outer space. Now it seems to have returned to some extent to its earlier style, and deals, perhaps in a more subtle way, with visions of the future and satire on the present.

The serious novel written in English has probably been dominated by American writers recently. Certainly Saul Bellow, John Updike, Norman Mailer, and Mary Macarthy enjoy higher reputations than many of their English counterparts. By coincidence several of the writers who emerged in England in the fifties and sixties were women – Iris Murdoch who writes strangely complicated novels with psychological and philosophical overtones, Margaret Drabble who writes mostly about the problems of intelligent young women in modern society, and Muriel Spark who covers a range from pure comedy to stark tragedy. Perhaps only one novelist, B. S. Johnson, has continued the tradition of experiment with the novel form and content. Few major writers seem to be

The Arts

emerging; one writer that might fall into this category is John Berger, until now better known as an art critic, whose novel 'G' has been acclaimed on all sides.

Serious drama in England has similarly not been of a particularly memorable standard. The group of writers known as the 'Angry Young Men' in the fifties are mostly still writing but few of them have added to the reputations they had then. Perhaps only Harold Pinter has gone from strength to strength, evolving from superficially realistic plays to plays of almost complete abstraction. Some minor playwrights have emerged: Tom Stoppard with entertaining plays based largely on verbal wit; David Halliwell with plays that present, first one character's point of view, and then another's; Peter Terson with lively plays intended as a kind of people's drama.

Facts
i) In 1974 the average English person watched television for 17 hours 51 minutes a week. The BBC comedy programme 'The Morecambe and Wise Show' was watched by 25 million people, the wedding of Princess Anne by 22½ million.
ii) Among the all-time bestsellers in England are Margaret Mitchell's *Gone with the Wind*, Thomas Hardy's *Tess of the D'Urbervilles*, and Enid Blyton's *The River of Adventure* (a children's book). One of the most unexpected bestsellers in recent years has been J. R. Tolkien's *The Lord of the Rings* (a fantasy about a mythical world).
iii) In 1971/72 The Arts Council, which is the Government body responsible for arts, allocated £1,640,000 to the Royal Opera Company, £1,118,000 to the Sadlers Wells Opera, £416,000 to the National Theatre and £295,000 to the Royal Shakespeare Company.

Points to Consider
a) Are the reading habits in your country similar to those in England? In what ways do they differ?
b) Why are crime stories and science fiction so popular nowadays? Escapism?
c) Are there any reasons why English literature should not be very remarkable at the moment? Or does one's own time always seem unremarkable?

Topic Ten

Dialogue 1 *Theatrical Conventions*
Listen to this conversation between three friends who have just been to see a play; then repeat it in small sections and discuss the points that arise.

CHARLES: I thought that was quite amusing.
CATHERINE: I suppose it was all right as comedy. But none of the characters had any depth.
PAUL: What do you expect from a comedy? A comedy doesn't need well-developed characters.
CHARLES: That's not really true.
PAUL: It's part of the comic convention not to have proper characters.
CHARLES: Yes, but everything's convention, isn't it?
CATHERINE: How do you mean?
CHARLES: Well the Greeks had the convention that all murders took place off stage; the Elizabethans had the convention that people talked aloud to themselves. You've got to judge a play in terms of its conventions.
CATHERINE: I don't agree; you don't have to know when a play was written to know whether it's good or not.
PAUL: You mean there's some sort of absolute scale on which you can judge works of art?
CATHERINE: Well in a way, yes.
CHARLES: All your absolute scale would do is reflect your own tastes and prejudices; there wouldn't be anything objective about it at all.

Talking Points
a) Do comedies need well-developed characters? Is it the same on television or in the cinema?
b) What are the current theatre conventions? Are there any universal conventions?
c) Can you have an absolute scale for judging works of art? Who could establish it and how?

Dialogue 2 *Detective Stories*
First read this conversation between two friends silently. Then choose parts and read it aloud. Finally discuss any points that arise.

ROGER: What's that you're reading?
SUSAN: It's a detective story.
ROGER: Who by?
SUSAN: Nicholas Freeling.

The Arts

ROGER: Who's he?
SUSAN: Oh he writes about Holland usually.
ROGER: Any good?
SUSAN: Well I quite like them. He gets across the atmosphere of Holland: you feel what it's like to be Dutch.
ROGER: Oh?
SUSAN: The actual detective part isn't very important; it's the characters and the way their minds work.
ROGER: Sounds interesting. I must say I can't stand those detective stories in which everybody is gathered together in the library in the last chapter.
SUSAN: Or they all appear in court.
ROGER: Perry Mason, you mean? I don't know; I find him quite readable.
SUSAN: Oh but it's just a formula. Every book has exactly the same pattern.
ROGER: Perhaps that's why I like it: I know more or less what's coming.

Talking Points
a) What makes a good detective story?
b) Why do people often apologize for liking detective stories?
c) Is writing to a pattern always bad? Have any 'serious' writers used this technique?

Activity 1 *Questionnaire*
Tick the answers that you agree with most.
1. How often do you buy a paperback?
a) once a week
b) once a month
c) once a year
d) never
2. Which of the following statements do you support?
a) Books and films should not be censored.
b) Books and films should be censored for moral and political reasons.
c) Books and films should be censored for some moral reasons, say violence and sex.
d) Books should be censored for political reasons.
3. Which of the following mass forms of communication do you regard as the most influential?

Topic Ten

a) television
b) newspapers
c) books
d) radio

4. Should the purpose of a play be to provide
a) an experience that is 'theatre' but not necessarily related to 'real' life?
b) a heightened illusion of 'real' life?
c) a religious, moral, or political 'message'?
d) none of these?

5. Which of the following do you think should not be allowed on the stage?
a) actors playing God
b) naked women
c) simulated sex acts
d) murders
e) satires on politicians
f) violence

6. Which of the following types of film do you prefer to see?
a) horror stories
b) thrillers
c) Westerns (i.e. cowboy films)
d) musicals
e) romantic adventures
f) another kind of film not mentioned so far

7. When you go to see a film do you usually go because of
a) the actors or actresses?
b) the director?
c) reviews in the papers?
d) the producer?
e) the subject matter?
f) the scriptwriter?
g) none of these?

8. If you were bringing up a child would you
a) let him watch as much television as he liked?
b) ration how much he saw?
c) allow him only to watch programmes for children?
d) never let him watch?

Activity 2 *The Film of Hamlet*

Panorama Productions Ltd have decided to make a film of Hamlet in modern dress. First they have to select a director; the following are known to be available:

The Arts

    Alfred Hitchcock
    Ingmar Bergman
    Ken Russell
    Francois Truffaut
    Satyajit Ray
The following actors are willing to play Hamlet:
    Richard Burton
    Paul Newman
    Jean Paul Belmondo
    Jerry Lewis
    Omar Sharif
The actress to play Ophelia could be:
    Jeanne Moreau
    Liv Ullman
    Julie Andrews
    Ava Gardner
    Sophia Loren
Discuss which would be the most suitable combination and whether anybody else should be considered. If there is enough time discuss the shooting of the famous opening sequence in which the Horatio sees the Ghost of Hamlet's Father, a photo of whom appears on page 40.

Activity 3 *The Silford Arts Council*

The Silford Arts Council have been given £2,000 to distribute to deserving arts projects. The following people have applied for money.

John Driver, a painter, is asking for £3,000 to live on while he completes his series of paintings on the theme of life in Silford in the nineteenth century.

Silford Comprehensive School are trying to start ballet classes and need £450 to pay for the teacher and equipment.

The Open Street Theatre want £1,200 to form a group to tour factory offices and factories to involve the community in drama.

Mr and Mrs Cardell-Williams are asking for £1,600 to set up a small pottery-making industry in their back garden.

The Silford Operatic Society need £500 to hire halls for their concerts and £800 to buy new instruments.

The Council asks the people to come and justify their projects and then has to decide how to allocate the money.

Topic Ten

Activity 4 *Photographs*

Photo 1   *The Boyfriend* (a musical)
Describe what they are wearing and where they are dancing. What period do you think this musical tries to re-create?

Photo 2   *The Forsyte Saga* (a television series)
Describe the people in this family portrait. Can you guess their relationships? What are the attractions of books and films that tell you the story of a single family?

1

2

The Arts

Photo 3 *Laurel and Hardy*
Describe what they are doing. What other famous pairs of comedians have there been?

Photo 4 *Harold Pinter*
Describe his face. If you didn't know he was a playwright and actor what would you say he did?

3

4

Topic Ten

Activity 5 *Short Stories*
The students are divided into groups of about the same size; they then choose one of the following genres in each group, think of a story, and discuss it among themselves. Finally each group tells its own story, every member of the group speaking for roughly the same amount of time.
1. Science fiction
2. Fairy stories
3. Romances
4. Historical stories
5. Detective stories
6. Spy stories
7. Stories of heroism
8. Sentimental stories
9. Biographies
10. Westerns

Listening *Walking out of Films*
Passage 1 Listen to this talk before looking at the questions. Then listen to it again as many times as you need to answer the questions. Finally discuss any points that arise and look at the written text.

Questions
Tick the answers that fit the passage best.
1. The speaker
a) often goes to the cinema.
b) seldom goes to the cinema halfway through a film.
c) seldom leaves the cinema halfway through a film.
2. He dislikes the animal film because it was
a) sweet.
b) cruel.
c) for children.
3. He walked out a) when
                        b) because
                        c) although
a fox was giving a hen a shampoo.
4. The characters in the country house presumably shot
a) films.
b) birds.
c) themselves.

The Arts

5. The speaker thinks that film critics are
a) usually right.
b) often wrong.
c) boring.

Discussion points
a) What films have you disliked so much you have walked out? What can the audience do about a film or play that offends them?
b) To what extent should animals be ill-treated to provide entertainment or food? Are circuses cruel? Perfume-manufacturers?
c) What are the functions of film critics? Do you find their reviews useful or amusing?

Written Text
There have been few occasions on which I have actually walked out of the cinema halfway through a film. The first time this happened I was watching a story intended for children about animals living in a small village, riding in trains, shopping, and so on; the novelty was that the animals were all real. It was a sweet little film till you started wondering how the effects were achieved and began to look for the wires and things that forced the animals to behave in such a human-like way. The moment which had me walking out was a scene of a fox giving a shampoo to a hen. The look on the animals' faces and the faint signs of blood that appeared in the lather were too much for me: how many hens died to make that particular sequence?

The other two occasions on which I remember walking out were both, curiously enough, when I had gone to see films that had appeared on some critic's list of the ten best films. Both of them were extraordinarily boring. In one the characters sat in a French country house, drinking and smoking and doing nothing except a little shooting; presumably there was a profound comment on life hidden somewhere in this but I for one missed it. The other was a re-creation, in slow painstaking detail, of the life of a soldier in the First World War; it told me more about life in this period than I had any wish to know. For two out of ten films to be boring must show that critics love being bored; I've never been to see the other eight.

Topic Ten

Listening *Reality and Television*
Passage 2 This is an extract from a live conversation about television, particularly about its effects on children. The speakers are: Richard Parry, a polytechnic student, Robin Bell, an audio-visual editor, and Vivian Cook, a polytechnic lecturer.
  Listen to the conversation before looking at the exercise. Listen to the conversation again as many times as you need to do the exercise. Then discuss any points that arise and look at the written transcript. There are two versions of the transcript, edited and unedited.

Exercise
Agree or disagree with these statements by saying 'Yes' or 'No'.
1. The first speaker, Richard Parry, thinks it is obvious what is real on television.
2. The second speaker, Robin Bell, suggests that even adults do not always know.
3. Richard Parry tends to assume that other people think the same way as himself.
4. The third speaker, Vivian Cook, was on a space show a few years ago.
5. He was surprised by the quality of the television picture of the rocket.
6. He believes that modern communication is miraculous.
7. He thinks children are not affected by violence they cannot understand.
8. Richard Parry agrees that people are being burnt all the time.

Discussion Points
a) Do you find it easy to distinguish truth from fiction on television? What do you think this could mean to children?
b) To what extent does one judge other people by oneself? Is this always bad or good?
c) Should violence be shown on television? When it's real, i.e. news programmes?

Unedited Transcript
RICHARD PARRY: I think you ought to draw the line between what is and what isn't rather more clearly than it is drawn now.
ROBIN BELL: Well I think you ought to be able to give a child um a clear answer and I'm not at all sure that very many

adults have a very well-defined line between truth and fiction on the the mass media.

RICHARD PARRY: Yes, I suppose I suppose that is true. I mean we I suppose it sounds very smug to say it but we do tend to perhaps er see other people rather along our own lines. And perhaps they're not. I don't know I mean . . .

VIVIAN COOK: I remember on one of the . . .

RICHARD PARRY: . . . they're fairly discriminating as a as a collection of people.

VIVIAN COOK: In one of the space shows a few years back that I I happened to turn on and there was this rocket zipping across the sky with sort of smoke belching from all directions. I thought 'Good heavens! How did they get a camera close up like that?' And of course because they'd they'd omitted to show 'simulation' at the bottom um er and it wasn't for five minutes that I sort of realised you know that they hadn't quite achieved such miracles of communication by that stage and um certainly the sort of ersatz um reality is a is a danger. But I think that um the the the other question of um are children affected by the type of violence and reality that one sees on news programmes and documentary programmes – you know the people being burnt in various parts of the world, and explosions and this, that, and the other um er I think that as far as I can see they really aren't as affected by that as one imagines and it isn't within their sort of sphere of existence.

RICHARD PARRY: No, I think that's that's that's very true.

Edited Transcript

RICHARD PARRY: I think you have to draw the line between truth and fiction on television rather more clearly than at present.

ROBIN BELL: Yes, you ought to be able to give a child a clear answer. I'm not sure that many adults are clear about the line between truth and fiction on the television.

RICHARD PARRY: Yes, I suppose that's true. I suppose we do tend to see other people as ourselves. And perhaps they're different.

VIVIAN COOK: I happened to turn on one of those space programmes a few years ago and saw a rocket zipping across the sky with smoke pouring out of it. I thought 'Good heavens! How did they get a camera close up like that?' But of course they'd forgotten to show the word 'simulation' at the bottom.

Topic Ten

I didn't realise for five minutes that they hadn't quite achieved such miracles of communication yet. This kind of imitation reality is a danger. But I think that the other question of whether children are affected by the type of violence and reality that one sees on news and documentary programmes – you know, people being burnt, explosions, this, that, and the other – I think children really aren't as affected by that as one imagines as it isn't within their experience.

RICHARD PARRY: No, I think that's very true.

Written Work
Write briefly on one of the following topics.
1. Serious fiction v. light reading.
2. Contemporary literature in my country.
3. Theatre for the masses.
4. Education through television.
5. The best film I've ever seen.
6. The arts and the government.
7. Why are the cinema and the theatre getting more violent?
8. A film review.
9. A letter to your favourite film star asking for his or her autograph.
10. A conversation between two friends discussing the book one has just read.